Challenging the Secular Culture

Challenging the Secular Culture:
A Call to Christians

Edited by Stephen M. Krason

FRANCISCAN UNIVERSITY PRESS
Steubenville, Ohio, U.S.A.

Franciscan University Press
1235 University Boulevard
Steubenville, OH 43952
740-283-3771

Distributed by: The Catholic University of America Press
c/o HFS
P.O. Box 50370
Baltimore, MD 21211
800-537-5487

Library of Congress Cataloging-in-Publication Data
Names: Krason, Stephen M., editor. | Conference on "Challenging the Secular Culture: A Call to Christians" (2015 : Franciscan University of Steubenville)
Title: Challenging the secular culture : a call to Christians / edited by Stephen M. Krason.
Description: Steubenville : Franciscan University Press, 2016. | Includes index.
Identifiers: LCCN 2015043023 | ISBN 9780996930512 (hardcover)
Subjects: LCSH: Christianity and culture. | Catholic Church—Doctrines.
Classification: LCC BR115.C8 C4135 2016 | DDC 261—dc23
LC record available at http://lccn.loc.gov/2015043023

Printed in the United States of America.

This book is dedicated to my and my colleague and
fellow contributor, Benjamin Wiker's, grandchildren:
Dante Maximilian and Juliette Evangeline Wiker

Table of Contents

Foreword

By Anne Hendershott

In *Lumen Fidei* (*Light of Faith*), Pope Francis cautions us of the danger in embracing idols instead of the light of faith in God—suggesting that that we are drawn to idols because they are "the work of our own hands," and can be used as a "pretext for setting ourselves at the centre of reality." Secularism is one of the idols that Pope Francis is warning us about, and on April 13-14, 2015, the Veritas Center for Ethics in Public Life at Franciscan University of Steubenville hosted a conference on "Challenging the Secular Culture: A Call to Christians." The scholarly papers in this book were inspired by that conference.

Pope Francis knows—as do we—that worshiping worldly idols will never provide us with a meaningful "journey" but instead, only "a plethora of paths leading nowhere." Each of the papers acknowledges that the path without God—the path of secularism—will lead nowhere. We only have to look at our corrupted cultural institutions as evidenced by family breakdown, public policy on abortion and assisted suicide, same-sex marriage, and a continued coarsening of our popular culture, to know that without the light of faith we have already begun to break down into the "multiplicity of our desires" that Pope Francis is warning us about. The following papers demonstrate that we are already on a path leading nowhere. But, rather than cursing the darkness, each of these essays provides a kind of road map, directing us back toward a different path—a path of light that disestablishes secularism as an idol to be worshipped or a religion to be practiced. Each of the following essays provides us with a way to recover a culture directed toward a traditional understanding about faith and morality—a way to rebuild a culture that will foster human dignity and individual flourishing.

In the first paper, James Kalb, a lawyer, scholar and author, echoes Pope Francis' admonition that with an idol like secularism, we are fighting something that cannot sustain itself. And, like Pope Francis, Kalb suggests that the reason it is unsustainable is because it is false. Beginning his paper with an example of what he calls the "insanity of the technocratic project," Kalb illustrates this "insanity" with the fact that the new form of the New York City Health Department asks new parents seeking birth certificates whether the "woman giving birth" is male or female. Kalb wisely points out that such a form is an example of this "technocratic project" that aims to "turn the social world into a sort of universal machine for the maximum satisfaction of preferences." Choosing our own gender, or race, or sexual orientation creates a world that, "recognizes no transcendent authority above it, no history behind it except the history of its own coming into being, and no nature of things beneath it that cannot be transformed technologically into what we choose."

For Kalb, the real problem with secularism is that we have "turned rejection of higher goods into a higher good and called it freedom, autonomy, choice or respect for the supreme dignity of every human being…treating each of us as a little deity whose wishes are divine commands that define moral reality, taking vindication of our equal divinity as the goal of political and moral life." Kalb writes that once we have rejected our faith in God, we have transferred our faith to provide the "religious basis of the moral passion behind such causes as inclusiveness and multiculturalism." For Kalb, rejecting secularism requires us to begin to "restore the normal way people apprehend what is good, beautiful and true…getting people to recognize obvious primordial universals, like the constitution of humanity as male and female." Kalb believes that eventually the technocratic society cannot work because "natural human ways of thinking and acting are still with us." He believes that it is "possible that people will grow tired of silliness and return to sanity without extreme crisis." But, he still maintains that we need a response on "multiple fronts and levels, and include attempts to make improvements, moderate evils and encourage new growth." For Kalb, we need more than principles: "We cannot fight something with nothing, so we also need to present an actual way of life better than the one around us."

Benjamin Wiker offers a glimpse of that "better way of life" in his paper entitled "Disestablishing Secularism by Re-establishing the University." Wiker, an Associate Professor of Political Science and Human Life Studies at Franciscan University of Steubenville and Faculty Associate of the Veritas Center for Ethics in Public Life, maintains that in order to disestablish secularism we must reestablish the university. He argues that since universities were central in the triumph of the secular revolution, then they should be equally effective in launching a counter-revolution. Demonstrating that the secularization process began in the Enlightenment as part of the strategy of elevating non-Christian religions so as to demote Christianity from its central place in the West, Wiker suggests that the modern university systematically denigrates Christianity and Christian students—it is actively hostile to Christianity. Since the social sciences as well as the natural sciences now authoritatively define our culture, Wiker maintains that we cannot challenge secularism in our culture without challenging, directly and deeply, the intellectual disciplines at the modern secular university that give secular liberalism its authority to transform the culture according to its characteristic aims.

Wiker points out that the establishment of secularism was only made possible by establishing the authority of a comprehensive materialistic worldview, one that was grounded in a materialist account of nature—and he calls upon faculty of philosophy and history departments, as well as biology, chemistry and physics departments, to call that materialist account into question: "Christians should therefore be better biologists, better chemists and better physicists, just as they should be more honest and thorough historians."

Likewise, in an essay called "Let Them Be Born in Wonder," Anthony Esolen, Professor of English at Providence College, calls upon us to reject the technocratic project that has resulted in the creation of the Common Core in K-12 education—what he calls the "Common Curse that has been visited upon a once free people of three hundred million by a few men of immense power and wealth, narrow learning, little faith, and no wonder." Recalling that Socrates, the "wisest man in the ancient world" knew that he knew little, and never set himself up as the sole instructor of youth, Esolen asks, "Why would any decent human being desire to intrude himself into the education of millions and millions of other people's children, overruling the parents, reducing them to clean-fingered serfs on the bureaucratic and technocratic manor?"

For Esolen, "[g]race builds upon nature, not upon madness…you cannot avoid the poison, the poison is everywhere….And it is demonic." Esolen warns us that the demons will not let man be: "They will not stop at engineering our food; they will engineer the feeding too….[W]hen 'transgressing' becomes a virtue, then ambition knows no bounds but those imposed by greater power." Drawing lessons from Shakespeare, Esolen clearly identifies the roots of our current dilemma: "They began by denying the goodness of the natural. They are now celebrating the evil of the unnatural."

The paper by Robert R. Reilly, U. S. diplomat, former Director of Voice of America, and author, entitled "The New Gnosticism of the Homosexual Movement and How to Restore Reality" extends the conversation begun by Kalb and Esolen by suggesting that the homosexual movement is "a form of gnosticism—a spiritually pathological, magical reconstruction of reality." Reilly argues that the active homosexual wants to say and believe that his actions are ordered objectively—and this would require the reconstitution of reality so that it will conform to his will and transform his subjective acts into ones ordered to objective good. To succeed in this endeavor, Reilly points out that the homosexual must relocate the source of good from "what is" to his own will—just as Pope Francis predicted in *Lumen Fidei*. Only then can the active homosexual successfully rationalize his moral misbehavior.

Reilly says that the notion of same-sex marriage—pushed so aggressively by the homosexual movement—simply disregards the unitive and procreative ends of marriage. It asserts a purpose for marriage that is *against* its ends.

Acting against the ends of marriage will destroy it: "This is the nihilism inherent in the homosexual movement." For Reilly, this nihilism is dangerous because the homosexual movement extends to all of reality: "It leaves nothing untouched in its unhinging of nature. Recognition of nature means acknowledgment of constraints…but this type of emancipation—from the human condition itself—can lead only to the supremacy of force."

Suggesting that the reason that the pro-family position has been losing in the same-sex marriage debates is because there has been a "lack of moral substance in its defense of marriage," Reilly concludes that "the issue of the immorality of sodomy and other homosexual acts has been abandoned. That is a terrible substantive and strategic error. Giving up on that basically gives the whole issue away because if sodomy is not wrong, then not allowing it to serve as the basis of marriage must be bigotry." Reilly provides a way to recover the moral argument on homosexuality: simply claiming that "one must forthrightly say and show that sodomitical behavior is against the 'Laws of Nature and of Nature's God,' and therefore it cannot be advanced as a right."

Allan C. Carlson, the author of "Cycles, Secularism, and the Prospects for Family Renewal" refuses to be pessimistic about our current cultural dilemma. Identifying four distinct cycles in the history of the family in America, Carlson, President of the Howard Center and Editor of *Family in America*, identifies cycles of strength and weakness regarding the family occurring in "remarkably consistent fifty year swings." Periods of strength are evident from 1630 to 1680; from 1730 to 1780; 1830 to 1880; and from 1930 to 1970. These periods of family strength were preceded by periods of serious cultural decline from 1680 to 1730, 1780 to 1830, and 1880 to 1930. Much of Carlson's paper focuses on the period 1930 to 1970 as he identifies some of the sources or causes of this era of renewal—with a special emphasis on the role played by the Roman Catholics in America in stimulating this episode of revival, both familial and religious.

Carlson's essay will give hope to those who want to revitalize the culture. Identifying five factors that helped encourage family renewal, Carlson points out that the foundation of family renewal in mid-20th century America began with political recognition of the family itself—starting with the Presidency of Theodore Roosevelt who was the first openly pro-life and pro-family president. Carlson points out that on birth control, Roosevelt labeled the practice the "capital sin" against civilization, one that meant national death. Carlson also points to the culture of "maternalism" that elevated the status of motherhood and worked to reshape American public policy to reinforce the traditional home. Also, Carlson demonstrates that this era of family renewal also enjoyed the encouragement of the popular media—a media that helped to create a culture that was supportive of the traditional family structure of a man and a woman coming together to form a family. Unlike today's degraded media that celebrates the "freedom" provided by unencumbered couplings, the popular media of the mid-century elevated families.

Sheila Liaugminas points out the importance of the media in her essay, "Media Matter: Shaping Public Opinion for the Gospel." Host of *A Closer Look* on Relevant Radio and an Emmy award-winning journalist with experience in both the secular and the religious media, Liaugminas understands the importance of the Word, and begins her paper with statements from Pope John Paul II, Pope Benedict and Pope Francis on the importance of the Catholic media, and the contributions that Catholics can make in the secular media. Pope Francis called the Internet a "gift from God" in his 2014 World Day of Communications Message. Liaugminas reminds us that media communication "has been and remains an important pursuit and focus in the life of the Church, going out to all the world to tell the good news, by all means possible." She also warns us that "when the media have been complicit in advancing false narratives about news events, and social media users launch campaigns to advance those false narratives, the falsehoods take on a life of their own and people are persuaded." Concluding her chapter she encourages us to become involved in the media: "from Facebook and Twitter, to blogs and emails and texts and letters…we have the power to influence countless others, through the expression of our words."

An important way to influence the culture is by helping to shape the material culture—the art and architecture we create. In "A New Renaissance: The Church as Patroness of the Arts," architect Duncan Stroik reminds us that one of the major ways that the Church influenced culture historically was through the arts. Sadly, that is no longer the case as during the twentieth century the arts moved away from the Church and found more appealing patrons in civic and private realms. Stoik maintains that there is a desire for traditional architecture, and if done right, "it will speak to future generations." He asserts that "[i]n order to influence the culture today, we need to re-embrace the Church's role as patroness of the arts, including painting, sculpture, architecture, music, drama and dance." He also cautions us that too often we have expected talented artists and architects to work for the Church for the love of it—we think of them as a commodity and choose them based on the lowest price. He says that "[t]his is not a recipe for creating a masterpiece that the world will notice….Great art takes great talent and it also takes time. And the only way an artist can afford to do great work is to spend the time necessary and be remunerated for it." Stroik suggests a way for the Church to reclaim its role as a patroness of the arts once again, and identifies three important initiatives that will enable the Church to promote a culture of beauty, truth, and life.

In an essay entitled, "Restoring American Law," Lawrence M. Stratton, an attorney and Director of the Stover Center for Constitutional Studies and Moral Leadership at Waynesburg University, identifies the challenge facing Christians and all Americans in our own historical moment as to "restore the original principles expressed in the U. S. Constitution." Stratton reminds us that the Constitution's structural protections against power concentration sought to "Tame the Prince" by dividing the powers of government. Stratton also points out, however, that "James Madison's theory that the division of powers within the government would protect liberty as the branches of government competed with one another as ambition would counter ambition has not worked as planned." Too often administrative agencies—run by unaccountable bureaucrats—have written the rules we now live by. The result has been that "unelected bureaucrats write ninety-nine percent of the federal rules by which Americans must live." The bills that are passed now are vague and open for interpretation. Stratton suggests the reason for this is that "[i]f a bill was too specific, Congress might have to bear the political cost if the statute were to become unpopular….[T]he President would prefer a vague or open-ended statute so that he or she could more readily rewrite it in the administrative rule-making process, covered by the political fallback of blaming Congress for the statute's ambiguity." To begin to counteract this practice, Stratton offers ways for citizens to begin to re-engage in discussions about the proper vision of freedom, liberty, and equality before the law.

Building upon Stratton's call for a return to the principles of our constitutional republic, the concluding essay in this collection by Stephen M. Krason, Associate Director of the Veritas Center for Ethics in Public Life and Professor of Political Science and Legal Studies at Franciscan University of Steubenville, suggests that "when we talk about restoring sound culture, it can rightfully be said that in many respects it involves restoring the cultural conditions of our Founding Era and—in terms of politics, law and constitutionalism—the principles set down by our Founding Fathers." In "Restoring Sound Culture and American Principles: The Different Dimensions of a Social and Political Response," Krason asserts that "the struggle to restore sound culture, then, is a struggle to restore reason….[W]hile there may be different approaches, strategies, and ways of 'facing off' against the secular culture and securing cultural renewal, their objective at bottom must be to get people to think correctly—or, perhaps to learn for the first time simply *how to think*" (his emphasis). For Krason, we are in a "crisis of reason" as the forces of the secular culture are "descending to an ever more irrational and destructive level and exhibit an ever more intolerant and oppressive posture." Krason advises that we need to "begin to forge a foundation for a restoration of our compromised American Founding principles and more precisely, the culture that helped to spawn them, and provides a number of things that can be done at the personal, family, and individual citizen level." While his suggestions at this level are uncontroversial, Krason offers a dramatic challenge for the political arena by proposing a complete overhaul in the way we think about politics.

Indeed, this final paper—in some ways, the most prescriptive paper in the collection—is a proposal for a "new kind of politics," one that is educative. Krason believes that in order to rescue a "collapsing culture," executive power may be especially crucial to upholding and restoring American constitutional principles. He maintains that, "even while we are witnessing a misuse and possibly unconstitutional use of executive power in the Obama Presidency, we should not shy away from the strong, even sweeping use—although within the Constitution and our traditions—of executive power to help rescue us." Drawing upon historical justification for very strong executive power in ancient Greece and Rome, Krason reminds us that when the Athenians got into trouble, they turned to the great ethical poet Solon and gave him near complete power. Rome gave similar powers to statesman and former military leader Lucius Quinctius Cincinnatus: "He assumed power just long enough to do his job, and then returned to the plow on his farm. Both men were notable examples of self-limited power to our Founding Fathers. George Washington was sometimes called the 'American Cincinnatus.'"

Concluding his essay, Krason provides a path for Catholics to take in recovering the culture. Calling on the Catholic laity to "step up to the plate," Krason writes that "a properly formed and informed laity has to take the initiative to challenge the secular culture and try to change it, they have to do the work of reforming—that is, *re-forming*—it in the social, political, economic, legal, and institutional realms…it cannot wait for the bishops, clergy, or Church bureaucracies to do this."

All people of faith are becoming aware of these challenges. They know that culture is worth fighting for, and they also know that they cannot wait for someone else to do the work of remaking our culture. Sociologist Philip Rieff cautioned us that we can never "get beyond" the culture wars: "where there is culture there is struggle." The work of culture is the matter of and manner of disarming competing culture. The following chapters provide a way to begin that work.

Preface and Acknowledgements

By Stephen M. Krason

Faithful Catholic and other traditional Christian scholars and commentators write a great deal about the corruption of secular Western culture and its many components: morality, social life, politics, law, the situation of the family, etc. When the idea for conference was conceived by the Veritas Center for Ethics in Public Life at Franciscan University of Steubenville, the thinking was that while critique—even trenchant critique—is often necessary, it is not adequate. Christians have to be careful not to just "curse the darkness." After all, one of the great theological virtues—which are the highest of virtues—is hope. It was in that spirit that the Center, founded in 2013, assembled the group of scholars, writers, and people of affairs whose papers appear in this book for its second conference the aim of which would be to consider what things need to be done—and, in fact, realistically *can* be done—to begin to change the secular culture. The conference on "Challenging the Secular Culture: A Call to Christians" took place at Franciscan University on April 13-14, 2015, and what emerged from it was this book of the same title.

To challenge and try to change the secular culture is no small concern. Not only are Christians called to "re-establish all things in Christ" (Eph. 1:10), but they increasingly have no choice in the matter as the culture—whether by its propagation of immoral public practices which inevitably impinge on the lives of Christians like everyone else or by its increasing affronts to religious liberty—threatens them and they must act to protect themselves. It is the hope of the scholars connected with the Center that this conference and book may spawn further such efforts so Christians can gather and reflect more and more how they might proceed in this troubling time and consider how they might "network" and coordinate their efforts on many fronts to engage, respond to, and when needed, confront secularism and the culture—in many respects, the "rotten fruit" it has brought forth—in the years ahead.

I want to thank Fr. Sean Sheridan, T.O.R., President of Franciscan University of Steubenville and Dr. Daniel R. Kempton, the University's Vice President for Academic Affairs, not just for their support of the Veritas Center, but indeed for being responsible for its formation. It is the aim of the Center to reflect on how Catholic social teaching and Christian thought generally can provide the framework to examine and address the crucial public and cultural questions of our time. Franciscan University, of course, is also to be thanked for its financial support that made both the conference and the book possible. I want to thank Dr. Anne Hendershott, the Center's Director who I am most grateful to serve under, for her wise stewardship of the Center and her support for the idea for this conference and book from the time it was first suggested to her. Many thanks are due to Dr. Jonathan J. Sanford, formerly Franciscan University's Associate Vice President for Academic Affairs, for his considerable assistance to the Veritas Center and his efforts in bringing to fruition the conference and this book, and for Dr. Sarah Wear, the Director of Franciscan University Press, for her support and assistance. Mrs. Carrie Libetti, my secretary who also wears many other hats at Franciscan University, deserves much thanks and praise for her usual top-notch handling of so much of the planning and details for the conference. I thank Joseph Zarovnik for his assistance with the conference and my son, Stephen M. Krason II, Eric Mammolenti, and James Sarlo for help in preparing the manuscript for publication. Thanks are also due to the Franciscan University Conference Office for their substantial help with the conference.

Challenging the Secular Culture

The Challenge Goes Deep

By James Kalb

The titles of the other papers in this book and the conference that brought it forth express the reason for mine, because they say how much is involved in challenging the secular culture.

To start with, an effective challenge requires us to disestablish secularism, which now amounts to a religion. That means radically changing the academy, the media, and the legal system, which inculcate that religion and define the social world we live in.

It also requires us to defeat, or rather, reverse the movement to normalize homosexuality and same-sex "marriage." That movement has been enormously successful and turned into a holy war against what now counts as heresy, the view that the body and sex have meaning independent of individual will and desire. Once we have driven back the progressive jihad on that front, and re-established an understanding of the distinctiveness and complementarity of the sexes, we will be in a position to restore the family as a reliable center of life, love, education, culture, and faith.

We are concerned with more than institutional matters, of course. The project is not going to go anywhere without regard to the aesthetic and imaginative side of life, so we also have to recover humane learning and renew art and architecture. So we will discuss ways of doing that as well.

Putting the pieces together, we are talking about overcoming those who determine the legal order and control public discussion, reversing incredibly perverse religious and moral commitments, restoring the normal way people apprehend what is good, beautiful, and true, and getting people to recognize obvious primordial universals, like the constitution of humanity as male and female, that have become invisible and incomprehensible from the standpoint of what counts as mainstream public discussion.

If you look at the magnitude of what we propose and the influence of those in favor and those against the project, the whole thing seems insane. We are saying we are right and everyone who counts is wrong about human fundamentals. In fact, though, the situation is not nearly so dire. From the standpoint of reality and the all but universal judgment of humanity, we are not crazy, what we are against is crazy, and not only is it crazy, but everyone knows it. So we are fighting something that in the long run cannot sustain itself because it makes no ultimate sense. In spite of appearances, we can be confident that victory will ultimately be ours.

What I would like to do here is present some thoughts on this situation, why it exists, why efforts to deal with it have failed, and what needs to be done. I will paint with broad strokes, and present what I hope is a somewhat coherent view of the matter. The view is likely to seem gloomy in spite of ultimate hope. When times are bad, though, it is important not to underestimate problems. Whatever I have done, I think I have avoided that fault.

I will start my account with a recent event. According to a news report, "A [New York City] Health Department form for new parents requesting birth certificates asks the 'woman giving birth' if she's male or female."[1]

This, of course, is insanity. But why do such incidents keep popping up, and not only happen but repeat themselves and constantly grow more extreme? The natural untutored reaction to such events is that they cannot really be serious, that they are weird anomalies that will go away if we roll our eyes and go about our business and forget about them. That does not happen, though. The situation only gets worse, the oddities become more extreme, common, and compulsory, and no one prominent seems able to argue against what is happening in a coherent way.

What does it all mean? Evidently, that there is a problem in the way influential people think about things that is basic enough to destroy their grip on human reality—that is, their common sense. The problem is altogether fundamental, so much so that it is hard to stand back and see it for what it is.

It seems to me that, at bottom, what we are dealing with is what might be called the technocratic project, the modern attempt to turn the social world into a sort of universal machine for the maximum satisfaction of preferences. As such, the goal is something extraordinary: a social world that recognizes no transcendent authority above it, no history behind it except the history of its own coming into being, and no nature of things beneath it that cannot be transformed technologically into what we choose.

That project has been growing up for a long time, and it has enormous intellectual and institutional support. It comes out of an understanding of knowledge and the world with its roots in the early modern period, an understanding that emphasizes measurement, mathematics, and mechanism, and accepts as real only individual subjectivity and objects of the kind studied by modern physics.

That understanding does not float in the air. It is associated with modern science and technology, and allied to modern forms of social organization: the modern state, with its extensive bureaucracy and unlimited claims, and modern capitalism, with its energy, innovation, and global reach, and its flexible organization that combines infinite complexity with simplicity and clarity of basic principle.

Those alliances give the project of technological rationalization an energy and power that express themselves in continual radical reconfiguration of social life. That process has involved replacement by technological methods of religion, tradition, and natural moral law based on natural ends and ways of functioning. The latter are treated as irrelevant human impositions on a world composed of atoms, the void, and human sensation. So instead of piety and inherited ways, people think they should rely on contract, marketing, money, and the decisions of supposedly neutral expert bureaucrats based on social and organizational science.

That situation provides a fundamental explanation for such developments as: the redefinition of marriage; the insistence on treating sexual distinctions as irrelevancies; the desire to obliterate national and cultural boundaries; abolition of the good, beautiful, and true as objective realities; and a view of religion as private mythology, psychological therapy, or secular social concern by another name. All those things are unscientific and irrational, so they have to go.

As the process has extended itself, there has been a growing tendency to view opposition to its further extension as evil. Since older understandings are now considered simply irrational, they have come to seem arbitrary, oppressive, and presumptively violent. That is why the Supreme Court asserts that the only real reason for wanting to keep the natural and traditional definition of marriage is a desire to injure people who prefer connections of other kinds.[2] Such an interpretation makes sense to people for whom it goes without saying that there are no natural patterns of human functioning that we should respect, and the social order—including institutions such as marriage—is simply a construction for the purpose of helping people achieve whatever goals they happen to have.

From the beginning, a number of thinkers have recognized that there is something wrong with the technocratic project and the understandings that lie behind it. Pascal, with his rejection of Cartesian certainty as the standard for all knowledge, was an early example. Such thinkers have pointed out that knowledge is more than measurement and mathematics, reason is more than adapting means to ends, and the world cannot be understood as a system composed solely of atoms, the void, mechanism, and human sensation. The attempt to understand it in such a way wipes out the possibility of meaning, and with it rationality. It also obliterates functional patterns and implicit goals, which are non-mechanistic features of the world that are indispensable for understanding many of its aspect—for example, the functioning of living organisms, including man.

Such theoretical problems become intensely practical when the technological outlook is applied to human affairs. Human society cannot flourish while rejecting natural forms and functions, like sexual complementarity, and particular ties, like common history, loyalties, and culture. All those things are necessary as a basis for durable functional relationships that cannot be understood mechanistically but are central to how we live. Such relationships include the nuclear and extended family, but also larger configurations such as religious groups, local communities, and the complex arrangements that make up the culture of a particular people.

Further, technology has no interest in ultimate goods but only in realizing whatever goals people actually chose. In the liberal form of technocracy, the one that has prevailed, the goals are those of equal individuals, so individual satisfaction becomes the ultimate standard for action. That is a problem, since social order cannot endure without willing acceptance of sacrifice and recognition of values transcending getting what we want. And in any event, people are not satisfied by satisfaction of desire simply as such. We live by understandings as well as feelings, so we want to know that our desires are justified and our satisfactions worth having. We want to live in accordance with some sort of ideal, and to see ourselves as participants in the order of things, however simple, odd, or confused our idea of that order may be.

The liberal form of technocracy has dealt with that essentially religious need by turning rejection of higher goods into a higher good and calling it freedom, autonomy, choice, or respect for the supreme dignity of every human being. Basically, it treats each of us as a little deity whose wishes are divine commands that define moral reality, and takes vindication of our equal divinity as the goal of political and moral life. That is the religious basis of the moral passion behind such causes as inclusiveness and multiculturalism.

The solution works for those who guide the system through their control of various business, government, and not-for-profit bureaucracies, whose positions and activities it seems to justify. It enables them to claim that their power is not power at all, but loyal and disinterested defense of the power and dignity of every human being. It also works reasonably well for their hangers on, volunteer warriors for "social justice," who can participate in the triumph of their ideal and palliate the boredom of a politically correct consumer society by moral preening and the joy of smoking out and hunting down dissidents.

However, the solution does not give people in general a practical ideal to live by. "Whatever you want to do is OK, as long as it fits in with the equally OK things other people want to do" is not an inspirational guide to life. Also, its open-ended insistence on equality and emphasis on satisfactions rather than conduct leads to a custodial state that attempts to eliminate the danger that ordinary people will hurt themselves or oppress others by depriving them of agency and training them out of the ordinary functional ways of thinking that are now denounced as prejudices.[3] The result is that their lives go downhill in the way described by Theodore Dalrymple in his essays on the British underclass[4] and Charles Murray in his book *Coming Apart*,[5] and dramatized by the recent finding that over the past couple of decades the average life expectancy of white American women without high school diplomas has dropped five years.[6]

Nor does the solution work for serious Christians. Its illogic rankles, and it seems a poor substitute for older, more coherent commitments such as local, family, cultural, and religious attachments, not to mention the transcendent goals of their own faith. For that reason they view basic aspects of what secular liberals call social progress as the destruction of everything they love.

So what to do? To fight the secular culture we need to fight the technocratic system whose culture it is and whose ways and interests it expresses. What we are up against is therefore something powerful and deeply rooted, and those carrying on the struggle have been handicapped because they have not kept in mind or often even recognized how serious the situation is.

Some, for example, have limited their opposition to opposing government and transnational actors in favor of corporate and national ones, an approach that leads only to a slightly different version of liberal technocracy. The Catholic Church has been more thoughtful, and recent popes have kept alive principles like subsidiarity and natural law that resist technocracy fundamentally. Nonetheless, efforts intended to further the goals of Catholic social teaching have usually emphasized finding common ground with dominant forces for the sake of participating in something effective. The result has been support for expansion of the bureaucratic welfare state and thus of technocracy. There continue to be distributists within the Church who propose the integration of economic life with ordinary human concerns through the devolution of economic power to families and localities, but theirs has been mostly a niche literary movement with little influence.

The deficiency of fundamental analysis has made the battle against technocracy mostly a matter of feeling rather than principle. People who dissent from it are usually those with strong concrete ties to family, faith, heritage, and community, so their opposition usually emphasizes symbols, practices, institutions, and authorities rather than theory. The battle has therefore been a battle of ideological progressives against instinctive traditional conservatives, those who favor further development of dominant trends against those who dislike many of those trends but lack an adequate counter-theory.

That has not been the whole story, of course, but non-conservative tendencies of opposition have usually been even less coherent. There have been anarchists, who reject technocracy because they reject coercive order in general, and various hippies, greens, and feminists who also tend in that direction. The usual effect of their efforts, though, has been to strengthen the technocratic liberal state, which claims to be a neutral protector and facilitator of all tolerant ways of life, over other social authorities, and therefore to strengthen what they thought they were fighting.

So the dominant opposition has been conservative and mainly instinctive. That opposition has taken a number of forms. At its least theoretical it has simply proposed moderation or rather foot-dragging: some new demand seems odd or goes too far, and we are not ready for it. That approach is obviously ineffective in the long-term. Other conservatives have put forward particular demands that tended to limit technocracy. Libertarians have tried to limit the state and opposed its alliances with large institutions, which is why at least in America they are counted as conservative. Populists have tried to maintain what seemed to them common-sense understandings and limit the power of large rationalized institutions in general. And social conservatives have tried to maintain the strength and influence of traditional organic institutions like the family.

Such efforts have failed, in part because trends have been so adverse, but mostly because they have underestimated how deep the problems go. Populism flares up but is easily co-opted and soon disintegrates for lack of stable definition and leadership. Social conservatives have succeeded in offering determined and sporadically effective resistance on particular issues, such as abortion and to some extent "gay marriage," but overall they have lost ground for inability to link those issues to a more comprehensive and enduring structure of concerns.

Libertarian free marketeers seem an exception to the general rule of failure, since the limits of bureaucratic administration and importance of private economic decisionmaking have become quite generally accepted among influential people. The overall practical effect of their victories, though, has been extension and rationalization of markets—globalization, big box stores, and fast food franchises in place of local and more personal arrangements—and a sort of soft socialism in which government retains overall administrative control, but places extensive reliance on exchange, profit, and crony capitalism as organizing mechanisms. The result, as illustrated by bailouts of financial institutions and the ability of politically-connected real estate developers to use public authority to take other people's property for their own use, is a regime in which private property may profit its owners but does not limit state power, support family life, or protect the independence of homeowners, small businessmen, or local communities.

Religious and intellectual conservatives have paid more attention to basic principles. The former have emphasized the continuing importance of sacred tradition, the latter of general intellectual and spiritual concerns that cannot be reduced to utility. "Ideas have consequences," they have told us, so they have emphasized the aspects of human life technocracy leaves out and the errors of thought that have led to the current situation.

They have lost, too. Religious conservatives are loyal to heritage. When their political and social heritage is fundamentally liberal, that is a problem. God, America, and freedom get all mixed up together, and the easy way to deal with difficulties is to gloss them over and focus on symbols and rhetoric. The usual alternative to the resulting religion of patriotism is to separate religion from other aspects of social tradition, a move that tends to separate it from inherited interpretations and natural law as well, and ends by assimilating it into whatever anti-traditional trends happen to be dominant. So the usual alternative to right-wing political religion is left-wing political religion.

Literary and philosophical conservatives are politically and intellectually scattered, and tied by their professional position to an academic world that has become, in America, a half-trillion dollar industry providing training, expertise, and propaganda for industry and government. As such, it is not a place where conservative thought can become something more than individual idiosyncrasy. In addition, both religious and philosophical conservatives have often focused too much on the ideal side of life, on faith, values, the inner check, the moral imagination, or whatever, without enough attention to more practical things, to political and economic organization and the need for authority that is more concrete than the general authority of tradition and reason.

Not only have conservatives lost the battles, but to all appearances they have lost the war. After the Supreme Court finding that opponents of "gay marriage" are enemies of the human race, Obamacare imposing an all but universal mandate to provide contraceptives and abortifacients, and given the principle of inclusiveness combined with that of everlasting mass immigration from everywhere—both of which are seemingly unquestionable in mainstream public discussion—there is very little room left in America for any recognition of the roots of social order in nature, transcendent principle, or particular history and culture. The latter are viewed as oppressive principles to be overcome for the sake of equality, rationality, and individual autonomy. The only principles of order that retain legitimacy under such circumstances are bureaucracy, contract, and technology.

Appearances are deceiving, however, since the triumph of technocratic liberalism means its destruction. It is based on a defective understanding of knowledge and the world that destroys good judgment in ever more radical ways. How can a society be governed effectively if those who govern it resolutely refuse to recognize basic human goods, relationships, and patterns of behavior? How can a society survive if in principle it abolishes marriage? And how can it deal with problems realistically if it forbids discussion of human differences, so that prominent authorities insist, for example, that all high school students pass two years of algebra?[7] Also, liberal technocracy depends on popular acquiescence and secures it by promises of eternally more security, comfort, and prosperity for everyone. It will not be able to keep those promises: borrowing money to give people what they want is not a plan that will work forever.

Most basically, perhaps, liberal technocratic society needs its ideals, because it depends on reasonably loyal and dedicated ruling elites, and the ideal of equal freedom that inspires them and gives them legitimacy will grow steadily less believable as the years go by and the system becomes less free and more divided by class. Nor is a coherent and public-spirited elite likely to survive in a diverse multicultural society in which there is ever less social trust and more and more of the elite's members view themselves as entitled recipients of compensation for claimed oppressions rather than disinterested providers of social protections and benefits for others.

To make matters worse, it is very difficult for present-day society to self-correct or moderate its tendencies. It has been remarkably successful in most of the ways it cares about, so it is not likely to see the need to do so. Its intellectual life is highly institutional and departmental and thus resistant to fundamental change. It is enough of a meritocracy, and offers big enough rewards, to recruit most of the talent. And it is based on an understanding of knowledge that identifies it with neutral expertise, of morality that bases it on the choices of equal individuals, and of human life that views society as a big machine designed to promote maximum equal satisfaction. These understandings disallow possible sources of correction—tradition, common sense, the *consensus gentium*, the everyday human ability to recognize patterns—as sources of prejudice that cannot be objectively demonstrated and must therefore be excluded from public discussion. The same understandings also ground our elites' claim to rule, and the claim that our society is infinitely superior to any previous society, so no one who matters will want to change them.

The predictable result of such tendencies is a radically cosmopolitan and therefore deeply fragmented society that lacks common faith and loyalties, a lack that will eventually destroy the mutual trust needed for any form of public reason. Under such circumstances both the technocratic project and free cooperative public life become impossible, so the basis of rule is likely to become some combination of cronyism, dynasticism, deceit, bribery, and force, badly disguised by an ideology no one believes in. What we have to look forward to is something like the "Period of Stagnation" in the Soviet Union (running roughly from the accession of Brezhnez until Gorbachev's *glasnost*), followed eventually by transformation into something quite different that takes better account of considerations the established system excludes.

The question for us today, then, is how to promote developments that favor such a transformation and also head off a post-Soviet style collapse into ethnic hatreds and mafia rule. I have presented a gloomy account that tends to suggest the present order will destroy itself by insisting more and more single-mindedly on its principles, and that must happen before a better world can arise out of the ashes. That story is clear and easy to present, and events may turn out that way, but we cannot know in advance what will happen. A technocratic society would not work if it were technological through and through, since some degree of common sense is always present and necessary, so natural human ways of thinking and acting are still with us. It is therefore possible that people will grow tired of silliness and return to sanity without extreme crisis. The repeated failures of predictions that will happen, as well as the intellectual and institutional causes of the system's persistence, do not prove a turnaround will never come. So our response must be on multiple fronts and levels, and include attempts to make improvements, moderate evils, and encourage new growth. Some of the other speakers may suggest initiatives that seem likely to be fruitful in that regard.

What needs emphasis, though, is that repeated failures show we need a deeper and more realistic understanding of the problems we face. Conditions are bad, and it may be quite a while before things get better or even stop getting worse. What we do must be guided by that recognition. Experience shows it does little good to push specific causes when the basis of public life is so radically defective. Few public figures understand the reasons behind our positions, such as natural law morality, so they think such reasons are stupid or worse. What we need above all, then, is a fundamental transformation of the outlook guiding discussion and a radical broadening of the range of considerations thought relevant. That is a difficult task, for reasons already stated, but absolutely necessary.

For that reason, we need to emphasize the *most basic points*, in our own thinking and in our public activities. In spite of respectable opinion, equal preference satisfaction is not the supreme principle of morality and public order. Indeed, that view is our basic problem. It follows that spinning our message to fit the understandings that guide public life will lose us every battle and certainly the war. A turn toward better things will require putting truth ahead of desire and technique, and presenting it insistently at every opportunity. To that end we have to find once again our own way of speaking, make arguments that go beyond the principles of freedom, equality, and tolerance that our opponents propose and find useful, and bring human nature and substantive public goods back into the public discussion. And we need to emphasize a focus on truth and loyalty above society and beyond practical considerations. In other words, we need God.

We need more than principles, of course. We cannot fight something with nothing, so we also need to present an actual way of life better than the one around us. If we want to tell people there is something amiss we have to show them something better. Also, lack of continuity has been a problem for movements of resistance to liberal modernity. Resisting something so big and successful requires continuity of effort and discussion, and movements of opposition have been sporadic and disconnected. Progressives dominate public institutions and represent the interests of those who run them, and that gives them a certain cohesion and staying power. Our efforts must also have the solidity that comes from a connection to enduring social formations. For that reason our best hope lies in emphasizing connections to concrete local communities that gain their strength from ways of life and thought that answer the needs of ordinary human life. To stand fast when times are difficult, such communities need a definite system of belief and standards of behavior, along with an ultimate principle of authority so disputes can be resolved and standards enforced. So we need both local religious communities and the Church in general.

In recent decades the leadership of the Church has emphasized common ground with a secular world that rejects traditional and transcendent authorities. That approach has not worked—the Church has assimilated to the world rather than the reverse—and it will be hard to make much progress until it changes. In a hierarchical Church there is a limit to what laymen can do to promote such a change, and it takes a while for a large institution to learn from experience. Even so, the logic of the situation and the natural tendency of institutions that are well founded to return to type eventually make such a change likely, and even those who lack authority to make basic changes can prepare the way for them. We can do so, for example, by developing our thought in books like this one and at conferences like the one it was based on, and by constantly making sure that our lives are all that should be expected of Christians.

To fight the war we also need soldiers. Opponents of technocracy are usually traditional-minded conservatives. Today conservatism makes sense not in the sense of attachment to existing conditions, but in the sense of valuing history, human nature, a settled orientation toward something transcending economic utility, and patterns and attachments—like family and particular culture—that are necessary for normal social functioning. Helping re-establish a connection to such things when that connection is radically weakened will require new forms of thought and action. That is a problem, because the capture of institutions by the forces of liberal modernity has made our soldiers mostly populist and alienated them from systematic thought. That is true even of Catholics, who in theory accept hierarchy and intellectual authority, since the attitude of Church leaders has made resistance to liberal modernity within Catholicism anti-institutional. That situation must change as well. Presumably it will if the leadership of the Church once again picks up the torch of resistance, so that authority and organized thought once again align with a more adequate understanding of reality than the one now dominant.

Finally, in addition to God, the Church, our own way of thinking, speaking, and living, and coherent communities to embody and carry forward those things, we need an ultimate goal to provide a focus for effort. Without such a goal we are likely to react to particular events in a way that fails to deal with the situation as a whole and in the end submits to general trends. Since truth is to be the guide, the best hope for the future would seem to be an orientation toward a renewed Christendom, perhaps in the form of a society in which Christianity has a status similar to that of liberal human rights today. Christendom may seem an unrealistic goal, but technocratic liberalism will not last forever, there is no rule for what comes next, and the outlook and way of life that best fits human needs and aspirations will have an advantage in a time of increasingly radical disorder. Christians believe Christianity does just that, and if they are right, they have grounds for good hope. They must always keep in mind that Truth itself will be fighting for them.

Notes

[1] Leonard Greene, "Birth Certificates Ask Parents If 'Woman Giving Birth' Is Female," *New York Post*, January 30, 2015, http://nypost.com/2015/01/30/birth-certificates-ask-parents-if-woman-giving-birth-is-female/.

[2] *United States, Petitioner v. Edith Schlain Windsor, in Her Capacity as Executor of the Estate of Thea Clara Spyer, et al.*, 133 S.Ct. 2675 (United States Supreme Court 2013).

[3] Theodore Dalrymple, *In Praise of Prejudice: The Necessity of Preconceived Ideas* (New York: Encounter Books, 2007).

[4] Theodore Dalrymple, *Life at the Bottom: The Worldview That Makes the Underclass* (Chicago: Ivan R. Dee, 2003).

[5] Charles Murray, *Coming Apart: The State of White America, 1960-2010* (Crown Forum, 2012).

[6] Sabrina Tavernise, "Life Expectancy for Less Educated Whites in U.S. Is Shrinking," *The New York Times*, September 20, 2012, sec. U.S., http://www.nytimes.com/2012/09/21/us/life-expectancy-for-less-educated-whites-in-us-is-shrinking.html.

[7] Barbara Jones, "In Controversial Move, LAUSD's Deasy Wants to Raise High-School Graduation Requirements," *Los Angeles Daily News*, "Education" section, May 5,

2012, http://www. dailynews.com/social-affairs/20120505/in-controversial-move-lausds-deasy-wants-to-raise-high-school-graduation-requirements.

Disestablishing Secularism by Reestablishing the University

By Benjamin Wiker

I must first make clear the assumptions and arguments that define the title, "Disestablishing Secularism through Reestablishing the University." I have argued for them more extensively in my book, *Worshipping the State*.[1]

Obviously, I understand secularism to be something that has somehow been established—established in a real, legal sense—as in the establishment of one religion as the religion of the state, but also in the sense of ideas and arguments established institutionally, as in the ideas and arguments of modern secular liberalism becoming established as dominant in European and American universities.

There is an important connection between these two senses of establishment. The latter is in great part the cause of the former; that is, it was largely through the establishment of secularism in the universities of Europe in the late 18th and early 19th centuries and then of America in the 19th and early 20th centuries, that secular liberalism became in the United States the government-supported, legally imposed, constitutionally-mandated official worldview functioning exactly like a state religion in the 20th and now 21st centuries.[2]

Therefore, in order to disestablish secularism in both senses, we must reestablish the university. Since universities were central in the triumph of the secular revolution, then they should be equally effective in launching a counter-revolution.

To make clear how comprehensive a task I am advocating—in particular, why the university is so important in the counter-revolution against established secularism—we may begin with a definition of secularism, or more properly, secular liberalism.

By secularism I mean modern secularism, the centuries-long attempt to remove Christianity as the dominant source of authority defining our understanding of God, nature, human nature, rationality, and the human good. At the strategic center of this secularization was, and still is, a thoroughgoing, this-worldly materialism that has liberated Western society from Christianity by destroying its foundational assumptions: that God, angels, and the human immaterial soul exist, that miracles are possible, and that there is an afterlife, heaven and hell where ultimate rewards and punishments are dealt out.

Undermining these foundations allowed for the secular liberation from Christianity's moral, intellectual, legal, and cultural authority. The successive and successful attempts at liberation from Christianity—in philosophy, in literature, in biblical studies, in theology, in political philosophy, in the social sciences, in drama, in law, in music, or in the materialist-defined sciences—together constitute the comprehensive transformation that drove forward the secularization in the West.

While secularization in each of these disciplines may have arisen separately, each with its own particular history, they are all gathered together in the modern university. All share one common feature: the desire to remove Christianity, and replace it by an entirely this-worldly, materialist understanding of reality unencumbered by Christian theological and moral dogma.

To say it in its most terse form, secularization *is* de-Christianization, that is, liberation from Christianity. That liberation is at the heart of modern secular liberalism, and at the heart of the modern secularized university.

I emphasize this last point because it is too often overlooked. Modern secularization is not simply or essentially the denial of the existence of gods. Historically, modern secularization took place *within* a Christianized culture; therefore, it defined itself primarily *against* Christianity, against the particular religion that it was trying to remove—not Buddhism, Hinduism, Islam, or some generalized theism, but Christianity. Secularism's struggle against Christianity therefore defined its positive form. Modern secularism is not defined primarily by the denial of the existence of God, but by the denial of the existence of God as understood through Christianity. From every disciplinary angle, the modern university is defined by that very denial.

This important fact helps explain why secular activists since the Enlightenment so often hold up non-Western religions for approbation, even while they attack Christianity. To use a contemporary example, it helps explain the very odd and otherwise baffling hearty affirmation and defense of Islam today by the secular left, even while it continues to attack Christianity as the source of evil and conflict in the world. As I just noted, the affirmation of Islam by secular thinkers is not new: it began in the Enlightenment as part of their strategy of elevating non-Christian religions so as to demote Christianity from its central place in the West. The modern secular university is heir to that tradition, effusively affirming every religion, including Islam, even while it systematically denigrates Christianity and Christian students.

I note these things to help us understand more clearly the depth of the challenge that faces Christians in our secularized culture, and hence, how difficult it will be to challenge secularism in turn. Modern secularism is defined by the desire to remove Christianity itself; that means that its assumptions, its structure, its goals are essentially constituted by the negation of Christianity, and this negation historically constituted the modern secular university.

That helps explain why too many universities today—not just avowedly secular universities, but the Christian universities that imitate them—are not just indifferent, but actively hostile to Christianity.[3] That hostility is secularism's negation of Christianity institutionalized, and hence established, in the various disciplines from philosophy, psychology, sociology, literature, religious studies, and legal studies, to the so-called hard sciences, biology, chemistry, and physics.

Since all of these disciplines now authoritatively define our culture, we cannot challenge secularism in our culture without challenging, directly and deeply, the intellectual disciplines at the modern secular university that give secular liberalism its authority to transform the culture according to its characteristic aims.

Let me offer a few quick examples to make clear how the secular intellectual revolution authorizes cultural transformation. If reductionist psychology is correct, and human beings really are entirely defined by DNA and neurology, then Christianity's claims about the human immaterial soul are entirely groundless, and therefore should not have any cultural authority, any more than the belief in fairies. If biology really can be reduced to chemistry, and human beings truly are an unintended effect of blind evolution, then giving human beings a special moral status is both arbitrary and unwarranted, and therefore has no place in law. If there is no natural ground to morality that provides a natural standard for law, then we are stuck with secular liberalism's positivist account of law where competing but arbitrary rights claims battle it out in a moral void defined only by utilitarianism and hedonism. If the American Psychiatric Association is correct that, contrary to 2000 years of Christianity, homosexuality is not disordered, but in fact healthy, and that gay marriage, including children however produced, is indeed as good or better than heterosexual monogamy, then Christian opposition to gay marriage is entirely irrational and unsupportable. If the modern historical-critical method is correct in eliminating miracles and reducing biblical studies to cultural and intellectual history, then again, scriptural authority at the basis of Christian arguments is without foundation.

We could continue with each one of the disciplines taught in the modern secular university—and, we must again add, almost all Christian or originally Christian colleges and universities—but the point should be clear enough. The modern secular university is unified, throughout its disciplines, largely by intellectual assumptions and approaches that, in one way or another, provide the authority for de-Christianization of culture. The secular culture cannot be challenged until that intellectual authority emanating from the modern secular university is called into question by an even more thorough and rigorous, discipline by discipline, deeply rational and systematic, set of counter-arguments.

To help us understand even more clearly why this is so—that is, why disestablishing secularism in the culture must occur, in great part, through disestablishing secularism in the university—we may turn to the history of the university itself.

It is not news, I assume, that universities were an invention of Christianity, specifically, of Catholicism in the Middle Ages. There is no need to go over this well-known historical fact except that it is a fact that is not well known at most universities, even and especially Catholic ones. In short, Catholicism established the university, and it did so long before modern secularism arrived on the historical scene.

That indubitable fact puts modern secular or secularized universities in an interesting predicament—or should put them in one. They cannot tell the true history of the very intellectual institution in which they so comfortably carry on their secular revolution because that would call into question one of the cherished assumptions of modern secularism: that Christianity is irrational, even anti-rational.

The truth is that the original assumptions of the university, as developed about 800 years ago by the Church and in a Christianized culture, are that human beings are rational, that the world in all its complexity is intelligible, that speech can be used as a real vehicle for communicating truth, and that the truths of the faith do not conflict with the truths of reason because the same God who made the intelligible world, the God Who created human beings in His image, also redeemed the world.

That is why the first universities taught the *trivium* and *quadrivium* as the foundation of all other learning—comprised by grammar, logic, rhetoric, arithmetic, geometry, music, and astronomy—before students could advance to higher-level studies, like theology. The assumption was that all study of truth leads ultimately to the source of truth, and so we should have no fear of seeking the truth wherever it is found on the natural level.

This education was the most systematic and wide-reaching the world has ever known. Far from attacking reason, the Church was the source of its unprecedented expansion in the culture. Prior to the invention of the university, only a relative handful of people would have access to this kind of education. But in the Middle Ages, not just a few hundred, but hundreds of thousands of people from all over Europe, and from all social classes, passed through Europe's universities.[4]

Moreover, secularist historians are fond of claiming that it was only in the 17th century that the intellectual Enlightenment occurred that formed the foundation of modern science. The truth is that the astronomical and mathematical accomplishments of the 17th century were possible only because of the European-wide spread of mathematical and astronomical knowledge in the previous four centuries.

But while universities started out as Christian, and were Christian for many centuries, they were slowly transformed in Europe through the spread of the Enlightenment's anti-Christian assumptions and arguments, so that by the 19th century, Germany was considered the home of the most prestigious universities in Europe and these universities were deeply defined by the most radical Enlightenment thought.

It is important to note that this radicalization in the German universities was spearheaded by the incorporation of the new critical scholarship in theology and biblical studies, that is, through liberalized Christianity.[5] By liberalized Christianity I mean one whose biblical and doctrinal foundations were being undermined by the secular philosophical assumption, championed in the 17th and 18th centuries, that the purely material foundations of reality make miracles impossible. This materialist assumption arising in philosophy defined the new approach to science, which in turn authorized what can accurately be called the secularization of scripture among theologians and biblical scholars: the systematic removal of miracles, the denial of the divinity of Christ, the denial of the resurrection, and the subsequent dismissal of all doctrines based upon them. Once the supernatural source of Christianity's authority had been gutted, secularization (i.e., de-Christianization) of all the other academic disciplines could proceed without obstacle. The comprehensive intellectual secularization then authorized, even demanded, the secularization of the culture itself.[6]

How does this connect to our own American culture historically? Given that America had no graduate schools in the early 1800s, but only colleges still defined by their Protestant origins and goals, Americans in the 19th century seeking Ph.D.'s went to Germany, the initial wave being those in the first half of the 19th century who were seeking theology degrees. They brought the latest radical thought from Germany's universities back to America even before the Civil War. In the latter half of the 19th century, successive waves of Americans seeking Ph.D.'s in other disciplines would return to our shores and founded American graduate schools based upon the German model and staffed them with newly-minted Ph.D.'s with radical Enlightenment assumptions.[7] In America, then, the secular takeover of our intellectual institutions was not gradual or modest, like a man getting a new hat, but abrupt and decisive, like a man getting an entirely new head, a secular head.

So it was that secular liberalism became established in our American universities. The essential assumption underneath this establishment was, again, that all of reality is entirely material, and hence, Christianity cannot be true. Since it is false, it is therefore a positive hindrance to society's progress. That is why Christianity had to be disestablished.

Disestablishing Christianity meant establishing or re-establishing each discipline upon the secular assumptions that had been guiding the radical Enlightenment secularist project in Europe for two centuries. The rejection of Christianity through secular materialist assumptions became the unifying goal of America's graduate schools, defining the meaning of intellectual progress.

However fractured and fractious the various disciplines have become in our modern secular universities, however deep their disagreements with each other, they agree on one thing, the one thing that defines the modern secular university: whatever is true, and perhaps nothing is true, at least we know that Christianity is false.

We have seen, in historical overview, how universities have moved from being a Christian invention, to an institution formed by the desire to remove Christianity from its central position defining our culture. In both cases, the university was at the very intellectual center defining the culture—in the first case helping alongside the Church to establish Christian culture, in the second case, acting as the authoritative intellectual source for wide-scale cultural secularization.

As long as secularized universities have that central intellectual, and hence cultural, authority, they will continue to act as one of the greatest challenges to Christianity—although challenge is not a strong enough description, since secularism aims at the destruction of Christianity.

And that is why secularism must be disestablished through reestablishing the university. Here, I do not mean merely starting a number of new Christian universities, because the real focus is not the university itself, but what is taught in it. Many well-intentioned Christians do not understand the depth of the secular intellectual revolution, and so often try to build upon assumptions that were designed to eliminate Christianity.

Merely focusing on starting a university that is staffed by Christians misses the true and truly daunting nature of the task that faces Christians. Since the modern secularized university has produced a prodigious amount of scholarship supporting its assumptions and goals, it is not just a matter of substituting Christians for secularists in the classrooms, but of overturning the intellectual authority of secularism by a thoroughgoing and honest critique of its assumptions, its goals, and all the scholarship that flows from them in each of the disciplines in the university.

That brings us to a question that I have purposely avoided—until now, that is. Does disestablishing the secular university mean explicitly reestablishing the university on Christian foundations? The answer is "No" and then, "Yes."

The answer is "No" because, as we have seen in the original founding of the universities, Christianity maintains that "truth cannot contradict truth" because the same God who created the world also redeemed it. Therefore—and here is the real challenge that Christianity should make to secularism—the honest and deep search for truth in any discipline will show that secularism is fundamentally flawed, both in its assumptions and its goals, and hence in significant aspects of its intellectual output.

But the answer is also "Yes." In the deepest sense, if Christianity is right about its foundations in God, nature, human nature, rationality, and the human good, then all honest and deep searching in the various disciplines will, over time, reestablish Christianity as the guiding light of the university. In a more practical sense, the answer is yes because it is only within the Christian university that faculty and students will have the freedom to challenge secularism.

But let us not forget this deeper sense. If secularism is wrong, then it must necessarily distort truth. If modern secularism really is defined, essentially, by its rejection of Christianity, then correcting its distortion leads back to the affirmation, directly or indirectly, of its antithesis—Christianity.

This reestablishing of Christianity at the heart of the university is not, I must make clear, a whitewashing of its history. Sometimes the truth hurts, but it is still the truth, and it must be taught.

Now I do not want this to remain a general battle cry of which I am the general, so I will offer some very particular ways in very particular disciplines by which some headway could be made in intellectually disestablishing secularism, and therefore reestablishing the university on its proper foundations.

Let us begin with a revolutionary approach to the teaching of history. Why don't we teach history as *what actually happened*, and begin this story with the history of the university itself.

The secular Enlightenment account of Christianity declares it to be the source of irrational darkness aimed at suppressing intellectual development. An honest and deep inquiry into the history of the university would have to investigate what precisely it was about the central doctrines of Christianity that allowed the birth and development of the university centuries before modern secularism arose. There is no other way to understand the origin of the university historically. But this investigation could not help but immerse students in history classes in a positive inquiry into Christian doctrines, which in turn could not help but undermine the secular assumption that Christianity and its doctrines are antithetical to reason.

But let us add the history of science to our agenda. Since the universities were the source of the developments in mathematics and astronomy that grounded modern science (and as many historians in the last twenty-five years have amply shown, modern science has its roots in multiple advances made in the Middle Ages), then teaching the history of science demands that we treat Christianity, not as the enemy of science, but as is actually the case—once we remove the secularist distortions and tell what really happened—its original historical source.

Students who study the history of science must then ask questions now forbidden to them in secular universities, beginning with what is it about Christianity, doctrinally, that we find it as the original friend, not enemy, of science? And even more embarrassing for secularism, what is it about modern secularism that made it bent on obscuring that fact in the history departments of its universities?[8]

Another promising area of historical investigation, in an effort to teach what really happened, is the history of warfare. One of the great battle cries of Enlightenment secularism was actually taken over from the ancient pagan, pre-Christian Epicurean philosopher Lucretius who claimed, early and often in his *De Rerum Natura*, that religion was *the* cause of war. In the Enlightenment, this was repurposed in the propaganda, all too believable after the Thirty Years War, that Christianity was *the* cause of war, and hence for the safety of society, we need to secularize the public square.

The difficulty with the Lucretian-Enlightenment thesis is that it is historically false. As I have detailed in my *Worshipping the State*,[9] when you study, on a world-wide basis, the history of warfare, you find that very little of the carnage is actually caused by religion in general or Christianity in particular. Rather, the most stupendous destruction of life has come either from areas not touched by Christianity (as in Oriental dynastic wars), or from nationalistic and imperialistic ambitions (as in World Wars I and II), or from essentially anti-Christian secular utopian bloodletting (as in 20th century Marxism). The Chinese dynastic wars of Three Kingdoms in the 2nd and 3rd century A.D. claimed 35 to 40 million lives; the Mongol conquests of the Middle Ages, 30 to 40 million; and Chinese dynastic conquests in the 17th century, 25 million. The nationalistic, imperialistic ambitions driving World Wars I and II took some 65 to 85 million lives. Communism extinguished some 100 million.

What about the Thirty Years War? About 7.5 million, and religious conflict was only a partial cause.

Many students and professors alike have no idea about warfare in pre-Christian times or non-Western places or for non-religious reasons. Ignorance keeps both from asking questions that embarrass secular assumptions about what really caused the worst of history's wars. Again, this is not to deny that Christians must shoulder—honestly and repentantly—their share of the blame for war, but it is simply false to assume that Christianity is the source of the world's worst wars.

This is an especially important point if we recall that the Lucretian-Enlightenment assumption is the foundation for the secularizing notion that, since Christians as religious believers are ever on the edge of bursting into full-flamed conflict, the church must be forced out of public life by the state.

The truth is, that "If you really wanted to separate what has caused the most wars from the state, it wouldn't be the church. You'd have to separate dynastic aspiration, ethnic rivalry, economic ambition, national and tribal identity, the desire for glory, the desire for luxury and a life of ease, technological power...the power of propaganda," and last but not least, secular utopianism "from the state—for these have been the overwhelming motives for war and the actual causes of its destructive toll in human history."[10]

What about psychology and the social sciences? Here, I would like to refer to Robert R. Reilly's *Making Gay Okay: How Rationalizing Homosexual Behavior is Changing Everything*.[11] As Reilly documents in significant detail, the secularist attempt to push the gay agenda, including gay marriage, depends in great part on psychologists ignoring or suppressing data that would undermine the attempt to normalize homosexuality. This normalizing enforces the legal and social destruction of the Christian, natural law understanding of sexuality.

To make some headway in disestablishing secularist assumptions and goals in this area, psychologists do not need to affirm the Nicene Creed or even the existence of the soul. They might begin by admitting that, as Reilly documents, the official change in the *Diagnostic and Statistical Manual* from classifying homosexuality as a disorder to affirming it as normal and healthy in the 1970s was the result of crude politicking by homosexual activists, rather than clinical evidence. Since then, psychologists are just as crudely pressured in academia and clinical practice to suppress or ignore evidence that homosexuality is self-destructive or reversible. What is needed for the disestablishment of this aspect of the secular sexual revolution is the academic freedom to investigate these very questions thoroughly, and publish the results freely. Reilly, helpfully, includes some of the research in this area,[12] but much more needs to be done, and the more that is done, the more that secularism will be disestablished in the university and the culture.

Speaking of disestablishment, there is much work that could be done in our law schools and political science departments in investigating the actual history of how it is that our First Amendment, or a very small snippet of it—the so-called Establishment Clause—became the judicial foundation for the national government's campaign to actively de-Christianize nearly every aspect of our culture. The source of the notion that "Congress shall make no law respecting an establishment of religion" *means* that the national government must actively erect "a wall of separation between church and state," is not the Constitution or the First Amendment itself, but the secularist view of law imported from Europe to our newly-established law schools in the early 20th century. It represents one more imposition of the Enlightenment notion that social progress means the removal of Christianity—in this case, one arbitrarily imposed on the text of the First Amendment, rather than derived from it, or from the Constitution.[13] Much the same could be said of the Supreme Court's invention of the right to privacy, and its use in pushing contraception, abortion, and homosexuality.

The point here is that a deep and wide cultural history that investigates the intellectual and social background of such immensely influential high court decisions as *Everson v. Board of Education*,[14] *Griswold v. Connecticut*,[15] *Roe v. Wade*,[16] and *Lawrence v. Texas*[17] reveals that the Court's power in redefining our culture is not based upon its alleged legal authority to interpret the Constitution, but merely represents all too plainly the abuse of intellectual authority for the sake of sake of carrying out a secular revolution. The academic unmasking of that abuse would go a long way in disestablishing the judicial power that academic secularists use as an intermediary to impose their views on the public through the judiciary. It would also go a long way in reestablishing the common law and natural law foundations of our legal system, if only by exposing to light, and hence to criticism, the utilitarian and positivist views that generally govern secular liberal legal theorists.

I mentioned above how important it was, in the secularization of German universities, to have the theological foundations of Christianity significantly softened, if not entirely eroded, by the modern historical-critical approach to the Bible. As a result, most universities have, at best, religion departments that treat Christianity as one more religion (neither true nor false), and at worst, biblical studies departments that actively destroy any possibility that Scripture contains any truth, revealed or otherwise.

Disestablishing secularism therefore necessitates a thoroughgoing critique of the historical-critical method in order to unearth its assumptions, as well as its hidden goals. In recent years, some headway has been made in this area, for the most part by philosophers and historians outside the discipline of theology.[18] In this case, disestablishing secularism academically requires an extensive analysis of the history of biblical scholarship, especially insofar as it was formed not by the demands of the biblical text itself but by the questionable secular assumptions that were brought to the text by exegetes. Since these assumptions were aimed at disestablishing Christianity culturally—as Scott Hahn and I argue extensively in *Politicizing the Bible*—questioning the caliber of these assumptions opens up the possibility of a renewal of scriptural scholarship, one that takes into account whatever is true and valuable in the historical-critical method, and leaves behind the corrosive secularist assumptions and goals.

Finally, we have seen that the establishment of secularism was only made possible by establishing the authority of a comprehensive materialistic worldview, one that was grounded in a materialist account of nature. If this materialistic worldview is not called into question academically—i.e., by the faculty of philosophy and history departments, and biology, chemistry, and physics departments—then *the* authoritative foundation of modern secularism will remain intact, and all that is inferred from that foundation in the various academic disciplines will remain largely impervious to criticism.

Here, disestablishment is a gargantuan and delicate task. What is *not* needed is the declaration that science is evil because it now happens to be, and has been for some time, materialistically defined. Nor do we need the simplistic rejection of evolution. Nor do we want to insert either souls or God Himself into perceived gaps in a materialist scientific framework. If what I have said above is correct—that Christians have nothing to fear from the truth about nature because God is the author of both nature and revelation—then the deepest, most thorough examinations of any aspect of nature should affirm, not destroy, faith.

Christians should therefore be better biologists, better chemists, and better physicists, just as they should be more honest and thorough historians. They should be able to take all of the latest advances in any science, and advance them still further, precisely because they believe, both through faith and through the ever deeper penetration of nature by human reason, that the world is both deeply ordered and deeply intelligible, indeed, made to be understood by human reason. Some headway has been made in this area, but much more needs to be done.[19]

Please understand that I am not listing all of these areas as scattered possibilities, but as indications of a yet-to-be-realized effort to reestablish the unified understanding of reality that originally and rightly should define the university. Again, I am not calling for the mere replacement of secularist approaches by Christian-friendly approaches, but for a kind of head-on intellectual confrontation, where (if I am right) the Christian understanding of reality will show itself rationally superior to the secular view that now governs the various academic disciplines.

It is in demonstrating its superior ability to defend and discover truth that Christianity will ultimately disestablish secularism and reestablish Christianity as the intellectual foundation of the university. Then, through its well-earned authority, Christianity will be able to disestablish secularism in the culture as well.

Notes

[1] Benjamin Wiker, *Worshipping the State: How Liberalism Became Our State Religion* (Washington, DC: Regnery, 2013).

[2] For overviews of secularization in of American academia as related to Europe, see the excellent compilation of essays by Christian Smith, *The Secular Revolution: Power, Interests, and Conflict in the Secularization of American Public Life* (Berkeley: University of California Press, 2003), and George Marsden, *The Soul of the American University* (New York: Oxford University Press, 1994).

[3] For a good overview, see Greg Lukianoff, *Unlearning Liberty: Campus Censorship and the End of American Debate* (New York: Encounter Books, 2012).

[4] Michael Shank, "That the Medieval Christian Church Suppressed the Growth of Science," in Ronald Numbers, ed., *Galileo Goes To Jail, and Other Myths about Science and Religion* (Cambridge, MA: Harvard University Press, 2010), 21-22. On the founding and curriculum of the universities see David Knowles, *The Evolution of Medieval Thought*, 2nd ed. (London: Longman, 1988), chaps. 13-14.

[5] See Thomas Howard, *Protestant Theology and the Making of the Modern German University* (New York: Oxford, 2006).

[6] For a full account of the intellectual revolution of the radical Enlightenment that preceded the German universities, especially the deep connection between the new historical-critical methods and secularization, see Scott Hahn and Benjamin Wiker, *Politicizing the Bible: The Roots of Historical Criticism and the Secularization of Scripture, 1300-1700* (New York, Crossroad, 2013).

[7] See my *Worshipping the State*, chap. 14; Marsden, *The Soul of the American University*; and Christian Smith, "Introduction," in Smith, *The Secular Revolution*, 1-96.

[8] For these and larger questions see Benjamin Wiker, *The Catholic Church and Science: Answering the Questions, Exposing the Myths* (Charlotte: St. Benedict Press, 2011).

[9] Wiker, *Worshipping the State*, 319-324.

[10] Ibid., 324.

[11] Robert Reilly, *Making Gay Okay: How Rationalizing Homosexual Behavior is Changing Everything* (San Francisco: Ignatius Press, 2014), chap. 7.

[12] Ibid., chaps. 5, 7.

[13] For a more detailed argument, see my *Worshipping the State.*

[14] 330 U.S. 1 (1947).

[15] 381 U.S. 479 (1965).

[16] 410 U.S. 113 (1973).

[17] 539 U.S. 558 (2003).

[18] For an extensive bibliography, and our own attempt to provide a deep historical criticism of the historical-critical method, see Scott Hahn and Benjamin Wiker, *Politicizing the Bible.*

[19] For how such an approach to the various hard sciences might look, see especially: Guillermo Gonzalez and Jay Richards, *The Privileged Planet: How Our Place in the Cosmos Is Designed for Discovery* (Washington, DC: Regnery, 2004); Simon Conway Morris, *Life's Solution: Inevitable Humans in a Lonely Universe* (Cambridge, UK: Cambridge University Press, 2003); John Barrow, et al., *Fitness of the Cosmos for Life: Biochemistry and Fine-Tuning* (New York: Cambridge, 2008); and Benjamin Wiker and

Jonathan Witt, *A Meaningful World: How the Arts and Sciences Reveal the Genius of Nature* (Downers Grove, IL: InterVarsity Press, 2006).

Let Them Be Born in Wonder

By Anthony Esolen

As I write these words, the window is open above me, and I can hear the cheerful call of a cardinal, and the barking of a dog, and can see a blue sky white-capped with the clouds, and the branches of possibly the world's tallest pussy willow tree, thirty feet high and poised gracefully near the warm south side of my house.

It is spring, finally, and the snow has melted from most of its hideaways in the yard. But the quick change in the season stirs my memory, and I am a small boy sitting at the kitchen table at breakfast, with my father reading the morning paper, mostly the sports section, while I am peering over the edge of it and reading it backwards and upside down, to find the baseball scores. There's the smell of burnt toast and butter and fried eggs. Also the sound of birds, the same kinds of birds that are singing outside of my window now, although at that time I didn't know their names.

Now comes the gurgle of a woodpecker, and I am walking on the old coal miners' paths in the woods with my dog. The snow is slowest to melt there, and is speckled with red buds from the trees. Your shoes often break through the crust into a squelch of mud. It is a good world.

I know that I have been writing about what young people ought to learn in school, and why the liberal arts, the free-making arts, so necessary for a free and fully human society, are fading fast. But I feel today that I should filch the words of Robert Frost and turn them to my purpose: "Something there is that does not love a school, That wants it down."

Suppose you consider that what is really important in a young person's life will be transacted within the walls of a school. Then my view of the "wind-walks" and the "silk-sack clouds" above me—well, what is it? If school is not *for* the human being and his encounter with a world inexpressibly beautiful and mysterious, which he feels as a gift and honors with his gratitude and wonder, most especially for that beautiful mystery we know as another human being, then what is school for? The cardinal, the willow, and the clouds, what are they? What can they possibly be? A pleasant diversion from what is called "real life," or a meaningless distraction, or raw stuff to dominate and use. Nor will the utilitarian stop there. Other people also become pleasant diversions, or meaningless distractions, or raw stuff to dominate and use. Children, as they say without irony or shame, are our most precious resource. Or they become conscripted accessories to that crime called a "lifestyle," like a finished basement or a time-share in Cancun.

I used to believe that unless people were "born in wonder," as the old motto for the famous humanities program at the University of Kansas put it, they would not be born at all. In a way that is true. Wonder, said Aristotle, is the beginning of the love of wisdom. It is not without passion, this wonder, though it is hard to describe just what the passion is. You hear a master play the lovely adagio of Vivaldi's lute concerto in C major, and you forget yourself; you experience something that can only be experienced in your flesh as a sadness that is not sad, and a joy that is not yet joy. "I am never merry when I hear sweet music," says Jessica to Lorenzo in *The Merchant of Venice,* as the two young lovers lean out upon the balcony at night, looking at the stars. "The reason is," says Lorenzo, "your spirits are attentive." For "the touches of sweet harmony" that stir our passions also bring them to the tranquility of order.

But what if you never know those touches of sweet harmony? Or what if your education has neglected them, or made them grotesque—the twists and strains of sour discord? Or what if everything you learn must be subordinated to the sound and fury of ambition? Be useful, or die? The money-lender Shylock had commanded Jessica to stop up the ears of his house against "the drum,/ And the vile squealing of the wry-necked fife." His descendant Scrooge shut the door of his counting house against the small children caroling "God Rest Ye Merry, Gentlemen." He who sings prays twice, said Saint Augustine, and singing is what the lover does. The cardinal outside my window is singing, and God has blessed him with a clear and tuneful throat. To sing is not simply to speak. To read a poem is not simply to gather information, or perhaps not to gather information at all. To behold a beautiful landscape is not to reckon up profitable ways to destroy it.

Lorenzo tells us what to think of the utilitarian:

> *The man that hath no music in himself,*
> *Nor is not moved with concord of sweet sounds,*
> *Is fit for treasons, stratagems, and spoils;*
> *The motions of his spirit are dull as night,*
> *And his affections dark as Erebus.*
> *Let no such man be trusted. Mark the music.*

Such a person is not "born in wonder." But that does not mean he is not *born.* Wonder is not the midwife. Something else is.

What would that be? I am asking what rough beast hammers its way out of the shell of a school in which there is none of the double-prayer that is singing, none of the double-singing that is prayer, no love for beauty simply because it is beautiful, no leisure to read a book because it is eloquent and wise, no honor given to the saints and sages and statesmen of the past, no humble deference to art, no understanding that all the week's working days are for the Sabbath, no boy lying on his back in the grass to look at clouds because they are clouds, none of the free-making arts, but all things transformed into belts and levers and pipes and molds, for the construction of workers, one single Common Curse for a nation that used to be free? If lust is the evil parody of marital love, if slogans chanted at a political rally are the evil parody of prayer, what is the evil parody of wonder?

We may not have one name for it, but I think Shakespeare can show us what it is. We see it at work in many of his plays. Shakespeare is not friendly to men who bustle about the world, making quiet wonder impossible for others. But I think it is in his finest romance of wonder, *The Tempest,* that he reveals the beast's face most clearly. Recall the situation. Courtiers from Naples and Milan have washed up on the shore of what appears to be a deserted island. They include three men of sin, Alonso the king of Naples, his brother Sebastian, and Antonio the usurping duke of Milan. Those three had conspired to supplant Prospero, the rightful duke of Milan, and to murder him and his infant daughter Miranda on the sly, setting them aboard a rotten tub of a ship, to drown at sea. But God has preserved Prospero and Miranda, and now, after twelve years, the conspirators, survivors of an apparent shipwreck, are on the island where Prospero dwells. Prospero himself has arranged it, by the use of his magic arts. So they are in his power.

They do not yet know that. As they trudge along the heath, the innocent old counselor Gonzalo, close friend of the exiled Prospero, remarks upon wonders. Every sailor to distant lands, he says, comes home with strange stories to tell, but "for the miracle,/ I mean our preservation, few in millions/ Can speak like us." He is trying to soothe the sorrow of the king Alonso, who believes that his son Ferdinand was drowned in the wreck, but Alonso is not ready yet to hear. Gonzalo sees in the island "everything advantageous to life." He marvels at the "how lush and lusty the grass looks." He observes that their garments, though drenched in the sea, "hold, notwithstanding, their freshness and glosses, being rather new-dyed than stained with salt water." He sees in fact a place that could be like Eden, or like the mythical golden age of the pagans, and he imagines being the ruler of it, not so much by means of ruling, but by refraining from rule:

> *All things in common nature should produce*
> *Without sweat or endeavor. Treason, felony,*
> *Sword, pike, knife, gun, or need of any engine*
> *Would I not have; but nature should bring forth,*
> *Of its own kind, all foison, all abundance,*

To feed my innocent people.

At which the wicked Sebastian and Antonio smirk. "No marrying 'mong his subjects?" asks Sebastian. "None, man, all idle," says Antonio, "whores and knaves."

Of course Gonzalo is daydreaming, and we know painfully well how necessary law and labor are. Antonio and Sebastian themselves are evidence that there can be no golden age so long as men of sin walk the earth. They are themselves the knaves they see populating Gonzalo's imagined kingdom. And that fits well with everything else they see or do not see. They laugh at the notion that their salvation has been a miracle. They do not see the green grass. To their eye it is but "tawny." Their garments, as they sense it, stink of brine and fish. Alonso is temporarily incapable of wonder because he is overwhelmed with sorrow; he can think only of his son Ferdinand: "O thou mine heir/ Of Naples and of Milan, what strange fish/ Hath made his meal on thee?" He will soon also be feeling the sharp tooth of conscience. But Antonio and Sebastian are rather peeved and frustrated than sorrowful. Sebastian's comfort for his brother the king is to blame him for the shipwreck.

Now, by this point in the play we know that the island is far more wondrous than even Gonzalo suspects. We have seen the mage Prospero, we have heard his conversation with the lively spirit Ariel, who describes how he "flamed amazement" upon the stricken mariners. We know that the ship was not wrecked. We know that "not a hair perished"—an echo of Saint Paul's reassurance to the mariners in the Acts of the Apostles. We know that the young Ferdinand did not die, but is safe and sound on the island. Most wondrous of all, we have seen the awakening of young love. I'll say more about that shortly.

Meanwhile, the spirit Ariel—the Hebrew name is masculine, and means "Lion of God"—enters the scene again, as Shakespeare's stage direction has it, "playing solemn music." We might say that music is just what the guilty Alonso needs, music that will soothe him to sleep and begin the process of his moral healing. Shakespeare often uses music in this way. When the child-changed King Lear is brought to the tent of Cordelia, the kindly physician orders both sleep and music. When, in *The Winter's Tale,* the innocent queen Hermione is about to be returned to life, Paulina, acting the part of a magician and stage director, calls out, "Music, awake her: strike." But here in *The Tempest* it does not at first appear that the men on the island hear the music at all. The good Gonzalo is the first to grow sleepy, then the rest of the entourage, and finally King Alonso. That leaves no one awake, no one standing, but Sebastian and Antonio. "What a strange drowsiness oppresses them," says Sebastian, and Antonio explains it away: "It is the quality o' th' climate."

We know that it is not that. It is Ariel's music, and Sebastian and Antonio themselves admit that if it was the climate, it seems to have had no effect on them. "I find not/ Myself disposed to sleep," says Sebastian. "Nor I," says Antonio. "My spirits are nimble."

Gonzalo, eminently capable of wonder, is asleep. Alonso is asleep. Sebastian and Antonio must believe that fools and idle dreamers are sleeping, while the "real world" we always hear of is bright-eyed and awake. Here we might expect Shakespeare to present us with all the clarity and strategy of the coldest Machiavellian, with a sharp eye for the main chance. But he does not. What he gives us, I think, penetrates into the disease of men who are not born in wonder. He gives us alternative dreams.

It is Antonio who is first to dream:

> *They fell together all, as by consent.*
> *They dropped as by a thunderstroke. What might,*
> *Worthy Sebastian—O, what might?—No more!*
> *And yet methinks I see it in thy face,*
> *What thou shouldst be. Th' occasion speaks thee, and*
> *My strong imagination sees a crown*
> *Dropping upon thy head.*

Sebastian at first appears not to know what Antonio is getting at. Indeed he accuses Antonio of being asleep:

> *It is a sleepy language, and thou speak'st*
> *Out of thy sleep. What is it thou didst say?*
> *This is a strange repose, to be asleep*
> *With eyes wide open; standing, speaking, moving,*
> *And yet so fast asleep* .

No, says Antonio, it is you, Sebastian, who are nodding, who are letting your fortunes fall asleep instead of seizing the opportunity. What opportunity? Kill your brother Alonso in his sleep. Antonio will kill Gonzalo, and Sebastian will be king of Naples. "What a sleep were this/ For your advancement!" cries Antonio. Sebastian has the rudiments of a conscience. "I remember," he says to Antonio, "you did supplant your brother Prospero." What of it, cries Antonio, and what of conscience? "Conscience is but a word that cowards use," cries that sleep-deprived dreamer Richard III, "Invented first to keep the strong in awe!" If conscience were a sore on the heel, says Antonio, he would wear slippers. "I feel not/ This deity in my bosom." So they draw their swords and prepare themselves to put Alonso and Gonzalo "to the perpetual wink," to that land of sleep whence no one in this life returns.

Do we see what takes the place of wonder? If only it were insensibility! Antonio does not hear the music, does not feel the pinch of guilt. But he does dream. Lady Macbeth walks in her sleep, because she is desperate in her guilt; Antonio sleeps in his walk, because he is beyond or beneath despair. She is beset with evil dreams of what she has done. Antonio blooms with evil dreams of what he is *going to do.* He walks with his eyes wide open into hell, like the witless beasts of the psalm. If wonder is the angel, what is the devil? If wonder is the elf, what is the orc? Shakespeare shows us: It is the soul's fascination before the terrible and fascinating vison of power, sheer power.

I am thinking again of the Common Curse, visited upon a once free people of three hundred million, by a few men of immense power and wealth, narrow learning, little faith, and no wonder, and I ask the question any sane man would ask, which is, "Why would you wish to do this?" The wisest man in the ancient world, Socrates, knew that he knew little, and never set himself up as a sole instructor of youth. Why would any decent human being desire to intrude himself into the education of millions and millions of other people's children, overruling the parents, reducing them to clean-fingered serfs on the bureaucratic and technocratic manor? I am again looking out of my window. The sun has declined well to the west, and shines with a yellow glow on the twigs of the willow. To be capable of wonder is to be capable of the simple gladness of letting things be. I do not want a better willow. I do not want that ugly thing called a "smarter planet." I do not want a planet at all. The song sparrows are enough. The ordinary duties and joys and sorrows of a human life are more than enough, if anything in this life of ours could be.

We have come, it seems to me, to a fork. It was once possible for a lad with no particular bent towards poetry to find his wellsprings of wonder in the earth he tilled, or the house he built; the same poet Hopkins who loved the "rose moles all in stipple upon trout that swim" loved also "landscaped plotted and pieced, fold, fallow, and plough,/ And all trades, their gear and tackle and trim." That is so no longer. Few of us are blessed with the humble corrective of good manual labor, with a barn to raise, cattle to tend, grain to mill, clothes to sew and mend. We live within the padded cell of high technology. It is not easy to smell the grass and the good earth. The arts and letters remain, and good books are cheaper than ever, but our schools no longer teach the orderly beauty of grammar, much less something as complex and subtle as poetry, and our universities have either abandoned the liberal arts or have wrenched them over to politics, where all is as a bacchanal of the worship of unfettered power. At such a point we must either return to music, and art, and poetry, for the sweet wisdom they can shower upon us, for their own sake, not because we are aesthetes, but because we are human; or we join in the nightmare of what Malcolm Muggeridge called Legend, noisy and shameless, with its bright lights, its wealth, its fame, its debauchery, and its madness.

Grace builds upon nature, not upon madness. Among people of past generations, books of wonder might have been spice; for us they must be antidotes. You cannot avoid the poison. The poison is everywhere.

And it is demonic. I am not reading too much into Shakespeare here. The greatest genius in the history of literature knew that the dream of power was demonic. Let me cite a small part of the chapter of Isaiah from which Shakespeare derived the name of Ariel, and almost all of the motifs of *The Tempest:*

And it shall be at an instant suddenly. A visitation shall come from the Lord of hosts in thunder, and with earthquake, and with a great noise of whirlwind and tempest, and with the flame of devouring fire.

And the multitude of all nations that have fought against Ariel, shall be as the dream of a vision by night, and all that have fought, and besieged and prevailed against it.

And as he that is hungry dreameth, and eateth, but when he is awake, his soul is empty; and as he that is thirsty dreameth, and drinketh, and after he is awake, is yet faint with thirst, and his soul is empty: so shall be the multitude of all the Gentiles, that have fought against mount Sion.

"I thirst," cried Jesus in agony from the Cross. His was the thirst of love; and when they tried to give him drugged wine on a sponge to deaden his pain, he spat it out. "Love never ends," says Saint Paul, and we might say that the thirst for power also never ends; it is insatiable. Why did Antonio betray his brother? Prospero says that he was "dry" for "sway," dry, utterly thirsty for power. The drunken monster Caliban will, later in the play, conspire with two drunken castaways from the ship to kill Prospero and take over the island. Their drunkenness is sometimes slapstick and silly, sometimes merely subhuman, often malevolent. But the drunkenness of Antonio, and of people fascinated by the cobra of power, is much more dangerous. They are far from wanting to let the willow and the cardinal be. They will not let *man* be. They will not stop at engineering our food; they will engineer the feeding too, and then the feeders. When "transgressing" becomes a virtue, then ambition knows no bounds but those imposed by greater power. Power and not love is the only thing that keeps demons in submission to other demons.

Hence we see why those who dream of power cannot endure the free-making arts, and cannot rest easy so long as some little boy in the world is wandering about the woods, looking for birds' nests. It is why they must transmute the poem to what they call "text," a chemical substance to analyze while fighting your way to the heights of wealth and power. It is why, years ago, what has become of the Girl Scouts demanded that all a girl's interests be evaluated in the light of a possible career. You could not get your patch for astronomy by learning about the stars and gazing upon them in quiet wonder. That was not enough. That was not even necessary. The one thing needful was that you talk to a professional, a woman, about becoming an astronomer. People who will not hear the beauty of a poem may be worse than deaf. People who will not see the dignity of a child kneeling in prayer may be worse than blind. Their ears and eyes may be sharp indeed, as Antonio's are sharp, in the mad world of power he inhabits.

There is another thing that the idolators of power cannot endure, cannot leave alone, and it too is central to Shakespeare's play. Prospero does not intend to kill his enemies, but he does intend to return to his dukedom in Milan, and to free Milan from the overlordship of Naples. The key to the plan is love. Ferdinand the prince of Naples is alive and on the island, and Miranda, Prospero's daughter—her very name, invented by Shakespeare, means "she who is worthy of wonder"—is of a marrying age. So Prospero brings them to an encounter. How so? By means of wonder.

When we first see Ferdinand, he is following the music of Ariel, who is singing a mysterious song about the quieting of the waves. But it does not appear to the youth where the music is coming from. It brings him a spiritual comfort, as he describes it to us:

> *Where should this music be? ' th' air or th' earth?*
> *It sounds no more; and sure it waits upon*
> *Some god o' th' island. Sitting on a bank,*
> *Weeping again the king my father's wrack,*
> *This music crept by me on the waters,*
> *Allaying both their fury and my passion*
> *With its sweet air. Thence I have followed it,*
> *Or it hath drawn me rather.*

Ferdinand believes that his father Alonso is dead, yet the music brings him a strange peace, as it seemed to still the waters. When it begins again, the words we hear suggest a death and a transformation that exceed the ordinary power of nature:

> *Full fathom five thy father lies;*
> *Of his bones are coral made;*
> *Those are pearls that were his eyes;*
> *Nothing of him that doth fade*
> *But doth suffer a sea change*
> *Into something rich and strange.*

"This is no mortal business," says Ferdinand.

And it is just at this point—at the dramatic union of the motifs of death, the changeless beauty of coral and pearl, the might of the sea, and a hint of wondrous change—that the most important event in the life of Ferdinand occurs. He sees Miranda; Miranda sees him. "I might call him/ A thing divine," says the girl, "for nothing natural/ I ever saw so noble." She is right. He is a man, not a spirit summoned up by her father, as she at first supposed. But what is a man? A little less than the angels, says the psalmist; made in the image of God, says the sacred author of Genesis. Not a monster ever thirsting for power; not the raw material for the nightmare seekers of power to work upon. Miranda is right, and so is Ferdinand when he addresses her: "Most sure, the goddess/ On whom these airs attend!" Before he knows her name he calls her by her name: "O you wonder!"

The encounter of a pure youth and a pure maiden—of all the natural things in this sorry world of ours, that may be the single one that the demons hate the most. The plotting of Sebastian and Antonio will be foiled; but politicians we will always have with us. They will live to dream again, and unless they repent of their ways and beg for the grace of God, they will dream their way into the nightmare called hell. Good books are our allies in the sweet cultivation of wonder, but they too are not the end. The natural world about us, made by the hand of God, is a powerful ally, that world of mighty tempests and waves, and the tiny homely wonders of wildflower and berry and mushrooms that spring up by the light of the moon. But the natural world is not the end. The marriage of a

Christian man and a Christian woman is "from the beginning," as Jesus says, and is an image of the end, the kingdom of God, which Jesus says is as a wedding feast that a king gave for his son.

That is why our educators must see to it that Ferdinand never meets Miranda—by making sure that there never will be a Ferdinand or a Miranda in the first place. They began by denying the goodness of the natural. They are now celebrating the evil of the unnatural. That is of a piece with the rest of the project. They began by disparaging the liberal arts. They now pervert them to ends that are crudely utilitarian or political. They began by worshiping nature as against man; they proceeded to ignore nature and to rob young people of the time and opportunity merely to be outdoors; they now immerse those young people in the unnatural, giving them hideous pictures to burn like caustic acid into their memories.

The Tempest ends with love born and love raised from the dead; the young love of Ferdinand and Miranda, and the genuine repentance of Alonso, who falls to his knees before Miranda to beg her forgiveness. Contemporary critics see none of it. They stand there like the cynical Antonio and Sebastian. Even Caliban the monster is reconciled to his master. But then Caliban, unlike the enforcers of the Curse, always was capable of wonder. When his fellow conspirators are spooked by Ariel's music, Caliban reassures them thus:

> *Be not afear'd: the isle is full of noises,*
> *Sounds and sweet airs that give delight and hurt not.*
> *Sometimes a thousand twangling instruments*
> *Will hum about mine ears; and sometime voices*
> *That, if I then had waked after long sleep,*
> *Will make me sleep again; and then, in dreaming,*
> *The clouds methought would open and show riches*
> *Ready to drop upon me, that, when I waked,*
> *I cried to dream again.*

It is a sorry time when Caliban shines as an exemplar of humanity. If we are to raise up human beings, from which the Lord may make saints, we cannot let our managers stifle the wonder in us. Surely a Catholic education can be at least as poetic as that misshapen "thing of darkness" on an unknown isle.

The New Gnosticism of the Homosexual Movement and How to Restore Reality

By Robert R. Reilly

"Ideas that are not true are dangerous to our souls and to our polities, whether we like it or not." - Rev. James V. Schall, S. J.

If Eric Voegelin were alive today, I think that he would see the homosexual movement as a form of gnosticism—a spiritually pathological, magical reconstruction of reality, or of a "second reality." Voegelin wrote that, "All gnostic movements are involved in the project of abolishing the constitution of being, with its origin in divine, transcendent being..."[1] Does this seem too extreme a charge to bring against the homosexual movement? As I will attempt to show, this is not about some sexual peccadillo that we can wink at and push off into a corner—it is a lie about humanity itself. Lesbian advocate Paula Ettelbrick proclaimed that, "transforming the very fabric of society... [and] radically reordering society's view of reality" is the goal of the homosexual movement. This is typical gnostic rhetoric about constructing a substitute reality.

Voegelin said that "Gnosticism... has produced something like the counter principles to the principles of existence; and, insofar as these principles determine an image of reality for the masses of the faithful, it has created a dream world that itself is a social force of the first importance in motivating attitudes and actions...."[2] Such counter principles are active and evident in every aspect of the promotion of the homosexual cause. And we have seen the power of its social force as it moved against the religious freedom protection law in Indiana in March, 2015. As a society we have moved from the point where the rationalization for homosexual misbehavior has been accepted as normative to the point where that rationalization will now be imposed and enforced, legally and by social forces at large, on everyone. If you speak out about this, you most likely will lose your job or your business and, most certainly, your social standing. You may be sued. You will become an embarrassment. These have become new forms of censorship, with a strong dose of self-censorship already at play. Libertarian journalist John Stossel said, “This movement has moved from tolerance to totalitarianism.”[3]

Voegelin analyzed the Nazi movement as a form of gnosticism. I do not think it is a stretch to point to Nazi Germany in 1935 as an analogy to current events and their similarly gnostic nature. That is when the Nuremberg Laws were passed, stripping Jews of their German citizenship and forbidding marriage between non-Jews and Jews. No doubt, there were still many fine and upstanding people in Germany at the time, including many Catholics, but from then on they had to keep their mouths shut about the Nazi racial superiority teachings because they were state law. I am sure there were many people opposed to the race theory of history who said to themselves, as people do today regarding homosexual “marriage,” “well, this is a losing issue. Let’s leave it alone and move on.” They were probably too frightened to consider what they were moving on to, just as people today avoid thinking about the consequences of the complete denial of reality involved in homosexual “marriage.” Anyone who thinks that we are involved in a denial of reality any less profound than that of 1935 Germany is kidding himself. Success for the homosexual dream requires the obliteration of the real and the removal of those who insist on the existence of reality.

Gnosticism does not accept the evidence of reality. It is not a matter of what gnostics do not know, but of what they refuse to acknowledge. Composer Igor Stravinsky wrote that “the old original sin was one of knowledge, the new original sin is one of non-acknowledgment.” It is the refusal to acknowledge anything outside the operation of the human will—most especially “the good” toward which the soul is ordered. The gnostic is not interested in conforming his mind to reality but in conforming reality to his wishes. Joseph Pieper defined self-deception as an unobjective perception of reality dictated by the will. It is the sheer willfulness of the homosexual movement that is notable. What are its consequences? Charles DeKonick said: “By a disordered love of one’s private good one rejects…the common good as something alien and judges it to be incompatible with one’s individual status…one freely abdicates the dignity proper to the rational creature in order to establish oneself as a radically independent whole.”[4] The common good is the casualty.

In saying that the homosexual ideology is an unobjective perception of reality, one should note at the same time that the active homosexual does not intend to perform a purely subjective act. He wants to say and believe that his actions are ordered objectively. This is what requires the reconstitution of reality so that it will conform to his will and transform his subjective acts into ones ordered to objective good. To succeed in this endeavor, the homosexual ideologue relocates the source of good from *what is* to his will. Only then can he successfully rationalize his moral misbehavior. This ideological operation is especially evident in the campaign for homosexual marriage. Because the use of the word "marriage" is a misrepresentation of the homosexual relationship that it professes to describe, the meaning of "marriage" must be changed and brought into accord with the homosexual relationship. To do this, homosexuals give marriage a purpose that is not congruent with its ends. The heterosexual couple wants, or has as its purpose, the fulfillment of the unitive and procreative ends of marriage. The homosexual couple does not have this purpose, and could not fulfill it. It has a purpose for marriage that is against its ends. The problem is that acting against the ends of marriage will tend to destroy it. This is the nihilism inherent in the homosexual movement.

Why is this so dangerous? The answer is: because the nihilism inherent in the homosexual movement necessarily extends to all of reality. It leaves nothing untouched in its unhinging of nature. Recognition of nature means acknowledgment of constraints. Charles McCoy gives us some idea of what happens when that recognition is withdrawn: "We have noted Aristotle's observation that human nature...may be said to be in a condition of bondage. This bondage produces in man a tendency to revolt and escape from his condition. But this type of emancipation—from the human condition itself—can lead only to the supremacy of force. Hence, true freedom, the 'political' freedom of man's very nature, is protected by an insistence on the primacy of theoretic (speculative) truth concerning man's nature and end."[5] McCoy wrote this many years before the arrival of the homosexual movement on the scene, but it applies exactly. The success of the homosexual movement can only be achieved by dethroning the primacy of truth concerning man's nature and end. By substituting the primacy of will for the primacy of reason, we may be sure that the supremacy of force will follow. Most likely this is what the late Francis Cardinal George had in mind in 2012, when he said, "I expect to die in bed, my successor will die in prison and his successor will die a martyr in the public square."

What is the standard we should use to measure things regarding man's nature and end, and how do we discern what is in accord with it or against it? Aristotle states that, "in order to find what is natural we must look among those things which according to nature are in a sound condition, not among those that are corrupt." In the *Politics* (1.5.1254a36-39), he says, "Thus the human being to be studied is one whose state is best, both in body and soul—in him this is clear." Francis Slade remarked that it is "clear because the end realized as form is present in its complete actuality"—meaning it has reached its perfection. Thus, because we know what a human being is in the fullest, we can understand what a privation is. For example, we can know with certainty that 20/20 vision is the best for the eye and blindness the worst. With 20/20 vision, the eye has reached its complete actuality. It is perfect as an eye. It possesses no potential to see better than it does. In respect to a man's sexual powers, which are unitive and generative by nature, the one whose state is best would be a man as husband

and father, just as for a woman it would be as wife and mother. This is how we know that homosexual inclinations are privations and that homosexual acts are disorders. It is not a matter of "who says." Homosexual behavior cannot actualize sexual potential because homosexual acts can be neither unitive nor procreative. Like a withered limb, congenital deafness, blindness, or a genetic predisposition to alcoholism, homosexual inclinations are not part of what a human being is in his essence. These are accidental, not essential properties. In each case, there is something missing that ought to be there. For instance, the limb ought to be able to move in its full strength, the ear ought to be able to hear, and the eye to see. The further a thing is from its perfection, the more defective or "corrupt" it is—just as blindness is the furthest defect of an eye with 20/20 vision. A privation of the good cannot itself be good. In fact, as St. Augustine said, evil is a privation of the good.

When Tim Cook, the CEO of Apple, announced that, "I'm proud to be gay, and I consider being gay among the greatest gifts God has given me,"[6] he substituted a privation of the good for the good itself. This is a metaphysical travesty. I wonder if an alcoholic, as he ambled into a bar, would say, "I'm proud to be an alcoholic and I consider alcoholism among the greatest gifts God has given me." Of course, if he is a *reformed* alcoholic and his struggle has led him to a deep spiritual life, he could consider the privation from which he suffered a kind of good in the same way that Alexander Solzhenitsyn said, "bless you, prison" about his horrible experiences in the Soviet Gulag. However, I do not think this is what Cook had in mind. His kind of inversion is typical of the homosexual rationalization, and was used by Cook in his subsequent attack on the Indiana religious freedom law. Cook averred that a law protecting religious believers from discrimination for their belief that sodomy cannot morally be the basis of marriage was itself a form of discrimination since it did not conform to the homosexual belief that homosexual acts are morally good. Soon it may be a condition of doing business in the United States that one accepts the moral legitimacy of the views expressed by Tim Cook—that a privation of the good is at least equivalent to the good of which it is a privation. This, of course, is an offense against the principle of non-contradiction, which is why Voegelin describes gnosticism as insane. Unless blindness is the same as sight, one cannot say that the use of sexual organs in ways unfit for either generation or union is the same as their use for generation and/or union.

Recall that Voegelin said, "In the Gnostic dream world . . . nonrecognition of reality is the first principle. As a consequence, types of action which in the real world would be considered as morally insane because of the real effects which they have will be considered moral in the dream world because they intended an entirely different effect. The gap between intended and real effect will be imputed not to the gnostic immorality of ignoring the structure of reality but to the immorality of some other person or society that does not behave as it should behave according to the dream conception of cause and effect. The interpretation of moral insanity as morality, and of the virtues of *sophia* and *prudentia* as immorality, is a confusion difficult to unravel."[7] It was certainly difficult to unravel in the debate about the Indiana and Arkansas religious liberty laws because of the successful substitution of the dream world for reality.

The imputation of blame not to gnostic immorality, but to the immorality of some other person or society as a whole is typical of homosexual apologetics. Here is a small sample from *The Washington Post* "Book World" review (January 31, 2014) of the book *Body Counts* by Larry Kramer. From the homosexual author comes the priceless line, made at a New York dinner party on the Upper West Side where a guest had said that infected gays get what they deserve: "One of these days you'll open the *New York Times* and read that I died of AIDS. When that happens, I want you to know it is people like you who killed me!" If someone had been speaking of the connection between smoking cigarettes and lung cancer, would Mr. Kramer have said that if he were to die of lung cancer, it would be their fault? 2014 also saw the release of an HBO film, *The Normal Heart*, a movie version of Kramer's play about the beginning of the HIV/AIDS epidemic. According to *Washington Post* columnist Richard Cohen, the film indicts President Ronald Reagan and New York Mayor Ed Koch for ignoring "a public health menace that needed immediate attention." Then comes the kicker: "The tendency then and somewhat still today was to blame gay men for their plight. The proposed remedy was to deprive them of their sex life—a remedy some felt was worse than the disease." This is part of the homosexual martyrology that it is easy to see the absurdity of, or what Voegelin called its "moral insanity," when it is transposed to other health problems.

Consider how this sounds: the tendency is to blame smokers for their lung cancer, and to propose a remedy—giving up cigarettes—that is worse than the disease; or, the tendency is to blame alcoholics for their liver disease and to propose a remedy—giving up alcohol—that is worse than the disease. According to this logic, the urgent public health remedy would be to find a remedy for AIDS that would allow active homosexuals to continue to behave promiscuously. However, the purpose of medicine is to restore an organ to health, not to allow its continued abuse.

On every pack of cigarettes, there is a warning that smoking causes cancer, and there are warnings on every bottle of alcohol that it may be injurious to your health. Why are there no warning signs regarding the sodomitical and other sexual behavior? It is likely far more dangerous for a homosexual to engage in sodomy than it is for him to smoke or drink. The Centers for Disease Control and Prevention provide the grim statistics. These figures confirm Joseph Costanzo's statement that "[t]he soundness of human nature is vindicated by the unhappiness and the disorders that ensue when society denies to it the true objects of love."[8] This comes at a high price even in terms of one's physical nature. The U.S. Department of Health and Human Services provides the most current data from Centers for Disease Control and Prevention, as of March 2012 ("MSM" means men who have sex with men):

> MSM accounted for 61 percent of all new HIV infections in the United States in 2009, as well as nearly half (49 percent)

> of people living with HIV in 2008 (the most recent year national prevalence data is available).
>
> CDC estimates that MSM account for just 2 percent of the US male population aged 13 and older, but accounted for more than 50 percent of all new HIV infections annually from 2006 to 2009. In 2010, MSM accounted for 61 percent of HIV diagnoses.

Might not these diseases be nature's way of tapping us on the shoulder to let us know that these activities are misuses of our bodies? Isn't it good news that, thanks to medical science, we now know which of our activities help engender these diseases, so that we can change our behavior? We seem to have gotten that message in regard to tobacco and alcohol, but not yet in terms of homosexual behavior. Putting a generative organ into an excretory organ is hygienically compromised and spreads disease. That is not the fault of Edward Koch or Ronald Reagan. It is the way we are made. *It is what is*. We may resent it. We may try to rebel against it. But we will suffer the consequences and, when we do, we will probably, as Voegelin predicted, blame others for it.

Changing the Vocabulary to Conform to Unreality: The Corruption of Language

None of these distortions would have surprised Voegelin, who said "the obsession of replacing the world of reality with the transfigured dream world has become the obsession of the one world in which the dreamers adopt the vocabulary of reality, while changing its meaning, as if the dream were reality."[9] Let us now examine some examples of the manipulation of language to construct a second reality. We shall also see that one cannot deny one part of reality without it affecting the rest of reality. To see the rationalization—the absolute denial of reality—in action, here is an online dialogue at Mercatornet.com with a homosexual (my remarks in italics).[10] I quote it at length because it shows so clearly the basis and nature of the rationalization and is very useful for diagnostic purposes:

> *Homosexuals cannot physically consummate a marriage—which means and has always meant coital sex. Isn't that obvious? How could you possibly deny it?*
>
> You ask how anyone could possibly deny that homosexuals are unable to consummate a marriage. It's easy. The word "consummate" flexes a little just as the word "marriage" has done. Consummation means something slightly different for a gay couple than for a straight one. Does it matter? Do we even need the word "consummation" in a gay marriage?

> *Simply call a giraffe a donkey and,* voila, *it becomes one! Magic! Just like homosexual marriage.*
>
> Yep. That's more or less the way it works, except that there has to be widespread acceptance of the word's new or expanded meaning. [This is why the rationalization must be shared by everyone.]
>
> *Do you really think your redefinition of reality actually changes reality? If so, you are living in a magical world—and I don't mean Disneyland. Welcome to the world of gnosticism and all its attendant spiritual pathologies.*

According to my interlocutor, nothing has a purpose. The eye is not for seeing, he says. It simply sees accidentally. He has to say this because he needs to establish that our sexual organs have no purpose, either. They are not unitive or procreative. Of course, if this were true, my interlocutor would not be here. Neither would any of the rest of us.

Can it be that every part of the human body serves an end—eyes for seeing, ears for hearing, tongues for tasting, noses for smelling—but that only one—the sexual organs—have no end? They alone are not directed to serve an end inherent in them? Or is it that man himself, in toto, has no end, and therefore neither do his sexual organs? This latter position would seem to have to be the price to pay for the purposelessness of one's sexual organs. The larger philosophical problem here is, of course, that if nothing has a purpose, you would not be able to know that it did not have a purpose. Purposelessness can only have meaning in the context of purpose.

In reaction to someone else's intervention in the exchange, the homosexual apologist said:

> All this talk about the "purposes" of biological organs is based in very narrow theological (teleological) concepts, not science. "Purpose," in the sense you meant it is the purpose intended by the designer, i.e., God. But evolutionary biology does not posit a designer, and so it does not posit "purposes" for body parts—least of all "single" purposes. Instead, biological organs and systems have functions—often multiple ones—that are not "assigned" or "designed," but that simply evolve through the processes of natural selection. This is not to say there are no "purposed" biological features, but they are "purposed" by the organisms themselves, not by a supernatural designer. [N. B. Aristotle said, "Man did not make himself to be man," but this homosexual thinks that organisms make themselves to be what they are.] The purpose that you have assigned to my sexual apparatus is *only* the purpose that *you* have assigned to it. It is not underwritten by any deity or "natural law." And then we

> come to sexual organs...their reproductive function is only secondary to their function in discharging arousal in our nervous systems. Most copulate not because they want to produce offspring, but because their nervous system needs release of accumulated tension (or arousal) brought on by contact with—or ideation about—other members of their species to whom they are attracted...Homosexual acts serve the same primary function for homosexuals as heterosexual acts do for heterosexuals. Arousal and release guarantee the smooth functioning of the nervous system...It is obviously not essential that semen end up fertilizing an egg.
>
> *But you obviously cannot deny that the purpose of the semen is to fertilize the egg.*
>
> Yes, I can deny that. I just did. Maybe it's hard to grasp, or maybe you're clinging to a popular, not a biological, understanding of the word "purpose." Biologists, when talking about how organisms evolved and how they function, do not use the words "purpose" and "function" interchangeably. You might say that a "purpose" is an "intended function." But "intended" by whom? Nature has no intentions. [N.B.: Aristotle wrote that, "Nature ever seeks an end," and that "Nature is a cause that operates for a purpose." (*Physics*)] Only organisms do. As I said, purposes are assigned or intended by designers. A medication can, of course, have a purpose because it is produced by designers (chemists). But organisms do not have "purposes" in this way because they are not designed or "purposed"; they simply evolved toward their present state...

Here is another example—this one from Amazon comments giving a negative reaction to a favorable review of my book, *Making Gay Okay: How Rationalizing Homosexual Behavior Is Changing Everything*:

> Where I disagree is with the traditional assumption that natural entities have "in-built purpose." This is a mere assumption, not something that has been discovered. The assumption results from projecting the way we create our own artifacts onto the creative activity of nature. Without this assumption the natural law case made against homosexuality fails. To truly support his argument, Reilly would have to PROVE that this age-old assumption is the actual truth of living things. (I would assert this to be an impossible task as living things are as ultimately purposeless as everything else in the universe.)

The purposelessness of the universe would seem a high price to pay for the rationalization of sodomy, but it appears to be a necessary one. Otherwise the rationalization crumbles. What is rhetorically interesting in these exchanges is the replacement of metaphysical and philosophical language with scientific, empirical language in the discussion of moral matters. The trick here is the substitution of efficient cause for final cause. This is easily done when the vocabulary is restricted to science, since science deals only with efficient causes. This bit of legerdemain is how the ends of nature are removed from the conception of reality held by the homosexual ideologues. Once the ends of nature are gone, man can substitute his own purposes for them. This operation is transparently present in the dialogues above, which is why they are so diagnostically valuable. One can clearly see what they are doing. Of course, this trick is as old as Machiavelli, Hobbes and Hume, and has served as the foundation stone of modernity. It is hardly a surprise to see it popping up in the rationalization for homosexual behavior. This also helps explain why the homosexual movement has such broad support from others who are not homosexuals, but who nonetheless share in the idea that nature is without ends in order to rationalize their own morally aberrant behavior.

As we have seen in these dialogues, the metaphysical trick of modernity compromises the integrity of language because words lose their relationship to reality, as means are no longer connected to ends—since ends no longer exist. Under this modern dispensation, words can mean anything we want them to mean. They are the tools with which the dream reality is built. The resulting perversion of language has reached new depths in the inverted use of words by the homosexual sub-movement known as "bug-chasing." Some homosexuals actually seek out partners whom they know are infected with HIV or AIDS because it makes the quest "more thrilling and dangerous." There is even a new book advocating the "chase" by W. C. Harris who, according to *Taki* magazine's Christopher Hart, is "a radical gay activist and Professor of Queer Studies and Early American Literature" at Shippensburg University, Pennsylvania. The book is *Slouching Towards Gaytheism: Christianity and Queer Survival in America*. There are many intriguing passages in Hart's review, but this one stands out. "'Breeding the virus in another man's body develops new kinships,' explains Harris (rather than, say, new burdens on health services), and they become one more couple in the 'bug brotherhood.' The one who does the infecting is called the daddy, the recipient the son, and such incestuous overtones are also very exciting, argues Professor Harris, for they too are transgressive, subversive, and liberating." Harris wrote that, "sharing viruses has come to be seen as a mechanism of alliance, a way of forming consanguinity with strangers and friends....Barebackers [those who engage in unprotected anal sex] see themselves as not just passing on a virus but as transmitting a cultural legacy....Through HIV, gay men have discovered they can 'breed' without women."[11] The transmogrification of language is complete. Disease is health, the family is infection, birth is bugs, and death is life.

The Application of Corrupted Language to the Construction of the Second Reality

This air of unreality also envelops the U.S. court system. When the U.S. Court of Appeals for the 9th Circuit rejected a bid to stay the ruling that invalidated Oregon's constitutional ban on same-sex marriage (May 19, 2014), Judge Michael McShane wrote in his opinion, "I believe that if we can look for a moment past gender and sexuality, we can see in these (same-sex) plaintiffs, nothing more or less than our own families, families who we would expect our constitution to protect, if not exalt, in equal measure." This is an extraordinary remark, which says, in effect, "if we can only look past what something is, we can see something else there." Indeed, we can. If, like my online interlocutor, we would only look past a giraffe's neck, we could call it a donkey. On the other hand, we might also wish to call the donkey a giraffe. This might be confusing, but at least they would be equal.

Families come from parents. You cannot look past the parents and still have a family because there would be *no* family there. This is what comes from looking "past gender and sexuality," which are the only means by which families are generated. Homosexual acts cannot generate families; therefore, their "families" *cannot* be the same. If there are children present in it, we may be sure that both parents are not. That is a lot to look past.

In Virginia where I reside, U.S. District Judge Arenda L. Wright Allen voided that part of our state constitution and those laws that define marriage as between one man and one woman as unconstitutional. Inaptly, Judge Wright Allen began her decision on February 13, 2014, by confusing the basic texts of the American Founding (since corrected). She apparently thought that the phrase that "all men are created equal" comes from the Constitution. It is, of course, perhaps the single most famous line in the Declaration of Independence. Its author was Thomas Jefferson. Judge Wright Allen appeals to this principle to endorse same-sex marriage on behalf of two lesbian and homosexual couples, who brought suit against Virginia.

What might Thomas Jefferson have thought of this use of the meaning of equality? We can more than guess. In 1778, Jefferson introduced the Bill for Proportioning Crimes and Punishment, which proposed that "Whosoever shall be guilty of Rape, Polygamy, or Sodomy with man or woman shall be punished, if a man, by castration, if a woman, by cutting thro' the cartilage of her nose a hole of one half inch diameter at the least."[12] We can safely conclude from this that Jefferson, who was actually trying to reduce the capital penalties for these crimes, would nonetheless not have endorsed same-sex marriage, the homo*sexual* expression of which almost invariably involves sodomy.

Why might Jefferson have proposed this bill to penalize sodomy and why did Virginia have laws against same-sex marriage? One would have to conclude from Judge Wright Allen that it was from sheer prejudice and that only now has the light dawned upon the court that this is unfair. In fact, she asserts that there is a lack of "any rational basis" in Virginia's exclusion of same-sex couples from marriage. In fact, she inaccurately states that "[t]hese laws limit the fundamental right to marry to only those Virginia citizens willing to choose a member of the opposite gender for a spouse."[13]Actually, they limit it much further than that, to exclude minors, the already married, the mentally infirm, immediate kin, and others. But why might this limitation exist in respect to same-sex couples? Judge Wright Allen never says, though she could have drawn upon several thousand years of Western and other civilizations to do so. Prejudice means pre-judgment—precisely the lack of *rational* consideration, which is essential to good judgment. The marriage laws of the United States, which have endured until recently, were not the result of prejudice, but of rational judgment. Was that judgment sound? We would never know how to answer this question since the reasons for it are missing from this ruling.

Here is part of what Judge Wright Allen neglected to say—even though it is part of the judicial history of the United States of which she should have been aware. In 1885, *Murphy v. Ramsey*, the U.S. Supreme Court decision which upheld the ban against polygamy in the Utah territory, eloquently put forth the "legitimate purpose" of marriage:

> For certainly no legislation can be supposed more wholesome and necessary in the founding of a free, self-governing commonwealth...than that which seeks to establish it on the basis of the idea of the family, as consisting in and springing from the union for life of one man and one woman in the holy estate of matrimony; the sure foundation of all that is stable and noble in our civilization; the best guarantee of that reverent morality which is the source of all beneficent progress in social and political improvement."[14]

However, Judge Wright Allen might object that this is exactly what same-sex couples want in marriage, as well. But they cannot have it—not for reasons having anything to do with nasty conservatives or with the law, but everything to do with how human beings are made. The ultimate, inbuilt end of sex is to make "one flesh," which is what happens in marriage between a man and a woman. Two becoming "one flesh" encompasses both the generative and unitive *nature* of sex. Only men and women are physically capable of becoming "one flesh." Only a unitive act can be generative, and only a generative act can be unitive—in that only it makes two "one flesh." That is why the unitive and procreative aspects of sex are essentially inseparable, and why they find the fulfillment only in the unique station of marriage.

What happens between a man and a woman in marriage *cannot* happen between two men or two women in a so-called marriage or otherwise. This is not a matter of *who* says, but of human nature, with every bit as much relevance to human flourishing and freedom as the "Laws of Nature and of Nature's God" to which the Declaration appealed for our independence. Change the meaning of nature at the level of marriage, and it will change the meaning at the level of the Declaration, with very profound consequences.

For homosexual couples, the marital act is physically impossible—the pieces don't fit—and the attempt to ape it through sodomy is incapable in any circumstances of generating new life. One thing that same-sex couples all share is a unique disability to express either the unitive or procreative essence of conjugal relations. For these reasons, among many others, common law has held *through the centuries* that marriage can be only between a man and a woman. Common law also held that if a marriage is not consummated, it could be declared to be a legal nullity. It is astonishing that Judge Wright Allen seems to be unaware of these things, though she shares her amnesia with Supreme Court Justice Anthony Kennedy and many others. In some states, entering into a marriage with the intent of never consummating the marriage is considered to be marital fraud. Since same-sex marriages cannot be consummated, one might say that Judge Wright Allen is complicit in perpetrating marital fraud, while disenfranchising the voters of Virginia.

Perhaps my favorite line from the ruling is that the "[homosexual persons] meet all of the legal requirements for marriage in Virginia except for the fact that they are the same gender." This is like saying that the only thing that prevents a giraffe from being a donkey is the fact that it is a giraffe. Somehow, I think that Judge Wright Allen would have failed Abraham Lincoln's famous quiz when he asked, "If you call a tail a leg, how many legs has a dog?" As if for Judge Wright Allen's future benefit, he answered, "Five? No, calling a tail a leg doesn't make it a leg." Does the principle of equality require that a dog have five legs, or that a giraffe be a donkey? Should we be required by law to say that tails are legs, or that giraffes and donkeys are the same? Is that equality, or the gnostic insanity to which Voegelin referred?

To say that something is what it isn't and can never be is an offense against reason, reality and sanity. Judge Wright Allen's decision is such an offense. Once you accept this basic unreality, it spreads, as is evident in Judge Wright Allen's opinion. She states, for instance, "Ms. Townley gave birth to the couple's daughter." But, of course, she didn't: the child was the daughter of Ms. Townley and the *father* of the child—not of her lesbian partner. Also, "Despite being deprived of the opportunity to participate in a legal adoption of her daughter, Ms. Schall is a loving parent." No doubt the love is not in question, but the child is not and could not be Ms. Schall's daughter, nor could she be its parent, as it is impossible for her to be the father.

One must also note that such children are deliberately made to be without both parents. Why is there no mention of the child's deprivation of one of its parents to make it possible for an unrelated person of the same gender as the mother to "love" it? A family is made to be broken, or rather broken to be made for the satisfaction of the same-sex spouse member who is not a parent. Too bad for the child who will never have a family with both parents, a father and a mother.

Judge Wright Allen tries to cover her sloppy thinking by quoting Abraham Lincoln in respect to slavery: "It can not have failed to strike you that these men ask for just…the same thing—fairness, and fairness only." Indeed, his fight against slavery, Lincoln appealed to Jefferson's famous phrase that "all men are created equal." However, Lincoln said something else that shows he, like Jefferson, knew that, while all people are equal, not all *acts* are equal—something which Judge Wright Allen, along with a number of other judges, has apparently forgotten. He said that one "cannot logically say that anybody has a right to do wrong." Both Jefferson and Lincoln found sodomy morally wrong. Also, Lincoln said, "Nothing should ever be implied as law, which leads to unjust or absurd consequences."[15] Like recent decisions similar to it, Judge Wright Allen's ruling is an act of will, not an act of law. It is an exercise of raw judicial power that shares in the coercive attempt to reconstitute reality for the benefit of those who require an alternate reality to rationalize their behavior. They want a right to do wrong.

Why We Are Losing

Why the pro-family forces are losing in court was explained, intentionally or not, by Judge Richard Posner in a 7th Circuit Court ruling (Sept. 4, 2014), in which he decided against the Indiana and Wisconsin laws restricting marriage to a man and a woman. He said: "The state [Wisconsin] does not mention Justice Alito's invocation of a moral case against same-sex marriage, when he states in his dissent that 'others explain the basis for the institution in more philosophical terms. They argue that marriage is essentially the solemnizing of a comprehensive, exclusive, permanent union that is intrinsically ordered to producing new life, even if it does not always do so….' That is a moral argument for limiting marriage to heterosexuals. The state does not mention the argument because as we said, it mounts no moral arguments against same-sex marriage."[16] This is why the pro-family position has been losing all along—from the lack of moral substance in its defense.

For instance, in 2009, California's Proposition 8, a constitutional amendment restricting marriage to one man and woman, was challenged in the U.S. District Court for the Northern District of California before Judge Vaughn Walker. Since the State Attorney General and the Governor had refused to defend their State's own constitution, other groups stepped in. They hired attorney Charles Cooper to plead their case. According to a *Wall Street Journal* profile, Cooper had "a record of championing conservative causes, including preserving gun rights and limiting affirmative action and gay rights."[17] He had been a clerk for a US Supreme Court justice and had worked in the Justice Department during the Reagan administration, eventually becoming the head of the Department's Office of Legal Counsel in 1985. He had more than 25 years' experience in government and private practice, and had appeared several times before the United States Supreme Court.

In a pre-trial hearing, the judge asked Cooper how the State's interest would be harmed if homosexual couples were allowed to marry. Cooper's answer was, "Your honor, my answer is, I don't know. I don't know."[18] This response was jubilantly pounced upon by advocates of same-sex marriage. "Opponents of gay people's freedom to marry still can't give a real answer to the key question,"[19] wrote the executive director of Freedom to Marry in the *New York Times*. It should have been an easy question to answer, but Cooper did not learn from his misstep. In a subsequent Supreme Court brief, he said the reason he did not know was because same-sex marriage is "a very recent innovation" whose impact "can't possibly be known now." However, it *can* be known if you know what marriage is. Just as you can predict the effect of counterfeit currency on sound money, you can know the effect of homosexual marriage on real marriage: it *devalues* it.

Why was Cooper not better prepared to make the moral case for marriage? The answer was given in 2014, when he revealed that, "My daughter Ashley's path in life has led her to happiness with a lovely young woman named Casey, and our family and Casey's family are looking forward to celebrating their marriage in just a few weeks."[20] How could one of the primary litigators tasked with the defense of marriage now espouse and celebrate homosexual marriage? Cooper stated that, "I told Ashley that what matters most is that I love her and she loves me." Indeed. However, as Edith Stein said, "Do not accept anything as love which lacks truth." Love contains an obligation to the truth—especially transcendent truths regarding the ordering of our souls to the Good. Is this Good not compromised by homosexual marriage? Love seeks the well-being of the other person. An unchaste act, which is any homosexual act, harms the person on whom it is performed and the person performing it. It is self-seeking, not self-giving. It damages both persons, regardless of their intentions. Is this not the fundamental moral question regarding it? Cooper did not address this issue because he said, "[M]y views evolve on issues of this kind the same way as other people's do, and how I view this down the road may not be the way I view it now, or how I viewed it 10 years ago."[21] Let us be clear as to how one can "evolve" in this way. There are two bases for it: one is called historicism, the other positivism.

Historicism claims that truth is conditioned by and contingent on history. In the sense that history changes, so does the truth. We can only see the "truth" of our own time, not that of the past or the future. There are no trans-historical truths rooted in the transcendent. In other words, all we really have are opinions. This seems to be the view of Justice Anthony Kennedy, who told a group of law students in 2013 that, "The nature of the injustice is you can't see it in your own times." The corollary of this has to be that you cannot see the nature of justice in your own times either. Where does this leave us? We are left with some sort of positivism, which states that truth is basically what we say it is, and all we can know is what we say. There is no metaphysical undergirding that can substantiate its truth or falsehood. By positing it, we make it true. Truth becomes the object of the will, rather than of reason. In his book *The Audacity of Hope*, President Barack Obama stated the grounds for his evolution, as he too evolved toward acceptance of homosexual marriage: "Implicit in [the Constitution's] structure, in the very idea of ordered liberty, was a rejection of absolute truth, the infallibility of any idea or ideology or theology or 'ism,' and any tyrannical consistency that might block future generations into a single, unalterable course." In other words, the truth does not set you free; the truth enslaves you. We shall see Cooper saying something similar.

Why did the pro-family forces not know that Cooper is an historicist and a positivist? If they had done their homework, they would have.

My late professor from Claremont Graduate University, Harry V. Jaffa, noted several decades ago that "the crisis of American constitutionalism—the crisis of the West—lies precisely in the denial that there are any such principles or truths [applicable to all men and all times]. It is no less a crisis in the heart of American conservatism than of American liberalism."[22] Without these principles Western nations could not "have a rational basis for the objective truth of their convictions instead of viewing them as arbitrary opinions or historical contingencies." (Jaffa was prescient in pointing out that this crisis existed in conservatism, as well.)

Curiously enough, Jaffa debated Cooper more than twenty years ago over these very issues. The debate exposed, at that early date, the grounds of Cooper's ability to "evolve." In ridiculing Jaffa's views of natural law as the foundation of the United States, Cooper wrote that, "The American people are thus enslaved to the 'moral and political philosophy' of the founders, powerless to redefine their 'legal and moral personality.'" Cooper asserted that, because it fundamentally limits what can be changed, "Jaffa's natural justice theory of constitutional interpretation is thus the very negation of the idea of self-government." No, it's not; it is its foundation. Without a basis in the "Laws of Nature and of Nature's God," self-government degenerates into willful majoritarianism—or what Benedict XVI called totalitarian democracy.

Very tellingly, Cooper was critical of Jaffa's view that it would be inherently contradictory to seek constitutional support and protection for "sexual orientation" because, as Jaffa said, "[S]odomy and lesbianism...are unnatural acts and, being unnatural, the very negation of anything that could be called a right according to nature." Why are such acts *unnatural*? Because they are neither unitive nor procreative—thus frustrating the two natural, inbuilt ends of human sexual powers. Only a historicist or a positivist could assert a right based upon these acts.

Cooper's clear lack of the natural law grounding made him a weak advocate for the defense of marriage. Here is what he suggested to the Supreme Court in the *Hollingsworth v. Perry* case as a defense of California's Proposition 8:

> But consider the California voter, in 2008, in the ballot booth, with the question before her whether or not this age-old bedrock social institution should be fundamentally redefined, and knowing that there's no way that she or anyone else could possibly know what the long-term implications of—of profound redefinition of a bedrock social institution would be. That is reason enough, Your Honor, that would hardly be irrational for that voter to say, I believe that this experiment, which is now only fairly four years old, even in Massachusetts, the oldest State that is conducting it, to say, I think it better for California to hit the pause button and await additional information from the jurisdictions where this experiment is still maturing."[23]

This is risibly weak. Wait for additional information? Cooper suggested that it was a *lack* of knowledge concerning the outcome of homosexual marriage that led to skepticism as to its soundness, rather than the moral knowledge that such an arrangement was against the "Laws of Nature and of Nature's God," and therefore could not possibly be advanced as a right. Since chastity is the moral principle of marriage, how could an unchaste act—such as sodomy or any other homosexual act—be made the basis of marriage? Something cannot be its opposite.

Cooper studiously avoided saying anything like this because, it would seem, there is no basis within his own beliefs for doing so. In acceding to homosexual marriage, Cooper reduced an objective good to a subjective preference, or rather conceded that a subjective preference is an objective good. The ease with which he did this demonstrates the lack of the very natural law foundation that he denigrated in Jaffa. Cooper appears to have been at pains to portray the issue of homosexual marriage as one of states' rights, avoiding, in fact not even raising, the question as to whether homosexual acts were inherently good or bad. This left him in the position of Stephen A. Douglas in the Lincoln/Douglas debates. Douglas said that the slavery issue should be left to the states to decide, as there was nothing inherently right or wrong in slavery. Popular sovereignty should reign. Cooper adopted an analogous position concerning homosexual marriage – it is a states' rights issue. However, homosexual proponents have taken on themselves the mantle of civil rights; they claim (inappropriately) to be Lincoln in this debate. This left Cooper in a sure-to-lose position—taking, analogously, the slavery position in an antislavery fight.

Here is Cooper's statement, posted on *National Review Online* (May 2, 2014), that confirms my characterization of his stance as like that of Stephen Douglas:

> The heart of our defense, from beginning to end, was the simple proposition that people of goodwill can reasonably disagree over whether marriage should be redefined to include same-sex couples, and that the Constitution, therefore, leaves resolution of that controversial public policy issue in the hands of the voters of each State, to decide according to their own social, political, and moral values, and does not place it in the hands of federal judges. Our position on the constitutional issue was thus entirely distinct from, and did not take sides on, the social policy issue. Indeed, in my initial appearance in the District Court, I stated that if the tables were turned—if California's voters had adopted gay marriage, as the voters of several states now have—I would be no less willing to defend their right to make that decision too.[24]

In other words, sodomitical marriage can be a positive good, so long as it is approved by a majority.

Not only homosexual marriage advocates, but our own supposedly pro-family legal counsels, like Cooper, are doing for sodomy what the Confederacy did for slavery—asserting it as a positive good, or at least leaving open the question as to its goodness. Contra Cooper, it is not objective truth that enslaves, but the unfettered passions. Homosexual marriage is the celebration of freedom without reason—using love as the excuse. It is the antithesis of the "moral and political philosophy" of the founders. However, true love is not blind, but is directed by nature toward the Good. As Lincoln said to Douglas in their debates about slavery, "[Judge Douglas] contends that whatever community wants slaves has a right to have them. So they have if it is not a wrong. But if it is wrong, he cannot say many people have a right to do wrong." (Lincoln, *Works*, III, 315)

Aside from Cooper, the problem from which many opponents to homosexual "marriage" suffer is a sense of moral illegitimacy—and this includes many Republicans. They have the right instinct that homosexual acts and "marriage" are wrong, but do not know how to express their view. When they are put on the spot to defend their opposition, they really have no way to explain it. Since they do not want to be embarrassed, they simply shut up. Most of these people have no background in moral philosophy or ethics. Like Cooper, they are products of our modern educational system which denudes the mind of any notion of natural law, which is the fundamental point from which homosexual "marriage" should be opposed, and replaces it with moral and cultural relativism. In their heart of hearts, these people probably wonder if they're not really prejudiced.

The reason for the kind of backpedaling exhibited in Indiana, whose governor could not adequately support the religious freedom protection law he had signed, is that no one wants to talk about what this is really about. The retreat to the position of defending religious freedom means that the issue of the immorality of sodomy and other homosexual acts has been abandoned. That is a terrible substantive and strategic error. Giving up on that basically gives the whole issue away—because if sodomy is not wrong, then not allowing it to serve as the basis of marriage must be bigotry. One must forthrightly say and show that sodomitical behavior is against the "Laws of Nature and of Nature's God" and that, therefore, it cannot be advanced as a right. If sodomy is wrong, then it cannot be the basis of marriage.

Why is there such silence on this subject from those who know better? We can find part of the answer in St. Augustine's *City of God*. In Book One, Chapter 9, he wrote: "We tend culpably to evade our responsibility when we ought to instruct and admonish them [the ill-doers], sometimes even with sharp reproof and censure, either because the task is irksome, or because we are afraid of giving offense; or it may be that we shrank from incurring their enmity, for fear that they may hinder and harm us in worldly matters, in respect either of what we eagerly seek to attain, or of what we weakly dread to lose." Today, the explanation for silence is more likely fear than irksomeness.

Conclusion

I do not have any cheery prognostications for the future. One of the reasons, as Voegelin said, is that, "Once a social environment of this type is organized, it will be difficult, if not impossible, to break it up by persuasion." It is clear that the homosexual "counterprinciples to the principles of existence" are succeeding in creating and imposing a dream image of reality on American society and, in fact, on the West as a whole.

This does not mean that the homosexual movement will succeed in the long run. Dream worlds do not last. Such dreams invariably turn into nightmares from which people eventually try to wake themselves. After all, reality still exists and cannot be banished. It will reassert itself one way or the other. How long that takes and how much damage the rationalization incurs in the meantime will depend partly on us. In other words, counter principles must be confronted with the real principles of existence. Reflecting upon his experiences in Nazi Germany where he had been imprisoned, Heinrich Rommen wrote: "When one of the relativist theories is made the basis of a totalitarian state, man is stirred to free himself from the pessimistic resignation that characterizes these relativist theories and to return to his principles."[25] He then went on to articulate those principles in his great work, *The Natural Law*, which could serve as an antidote to our present troubles from relativist theories. Like him, we must stir ourselves. In respect to the issue of natural law and natural reason in our day and age, Msgr. Robert Sokolowski counsels, "we have to restore the very concept of natural ends…." We have the means at hand to do this from our own country's foundation: they are called "the Laws of Nature and of Nature's God." This restoration is also necessary for the reestablishment of the integrity of language—so that words are reconnected with reality. For Joseph Pieper, according to Fr. James Schall, "the essential thing in philosophy is that not one single element of reality be suppressed or concealed—not one element of that unfathomable reality the vision of which is synonymous with the concept of 'truth.'" In other words, tell the truth, the whole truth, and be willing to pay the price that will exact.

Speaking of Solzhenitsyn and the experiences of spiritual recovery in Soviet camps, Gerhart Niemeyer, said, "These examples teach that 'a return' is possible, but also that no return may be possible without something like an annihilating situation…no recovery of order can be had by a merely intellectual *tour de force*: nothing short of a soul-shaking experience can stir up the ashes of lost truth."[26] We may be approaching such an annihilating situation. Rather than letting such a prospect depress us, we should see and prepare for it as an opportunity for the recovery of order. Cardinal George's full remarks about his successor dying in prison, and his successor dying a martyr, ended with this sentence, "His successor will pick up the shards of a ruined society and slowly help rebuild civilization, as the church has done so often in human history."[27]

I close with these comforting words from Eric Voegelin: "The closure of the soul in modern gnosticism can repress the truth of the soul, but it cannot remove the soul and its transcendence from the structure of reality."[28] The flight from reality cannot last forever. It will surely fail. We can help make sure it does by something as simple as telling the truth.

Notes

[1] Eric Voegelin, *Science, Politics, and Gnosticism: Two Essays* (Chicago: Henry Regnery, 1968), 99-100.

[2] Eric Voegelin, *The New Science of Politics* (Chicago, University of Chicago Press, 1952), 167.

[3] "Fox's Stoessel: Gay Marriage Movement Going from 'Tolerance to Totalitarianism,'" http://www.mediaite.com/tv/foxs-stossel-gay-marriage-movement-going-from-tolerance-to-totalitarianism/; Internet; accessed April 1, 2015.

[4] Cited in Charles N. R. McCoy, *The Structure of Political Thought: A Study in the History of Political Ideas* (New York, McGraw-Hill book Company, 1963), 201.

[5] Ibid, 47-48.

[6] Quoted at: http://www.bloomberg.com/news/articles/2014-10-30/tim-cook-speaks-up; Internet; accessed April 7, 2015.

[7] Eric Voegelin, *The New Science of Politics* (Chicago: University of Chicago Press, 1952), 169-70.

[8] Joseph Costanzo, "Catholic Politeia," *Fordham Law Review*, vol. 21, no. 2: 117.

[9] Eric Voegelin, *Modernity Without Restraint: The Political Religions, The New Science of Politics, and Science, Politics, and Gnosticism* (*Collected Works*, vol. 5), University of Missouri, 1999), 226.

[10] See: Robert R. Reilly, "Love in a Time of Unreality" (May 22, 2014), http://www.mercatornet.com/conjugality/view/love_in_a_time_of_unreality/14111.

[11] Christopher Hart, "A New Breed of Breeder," *Taki's Magazine,* March 28, 2014; http://takimag.com/article/a_new_breed_of_breeder_christopher_hart/print#axzz3Wa5vaVPm; Internet; accessed March 28, 2015

[12] Gaye Wilson, "Bill 64," *Thomas Jefferson Encyclopedia*, Monticello.org, http://www.monticello.org/site/research-and-collections/bill-64; Internet; accessed July 31, 2013.

[13] U.S. District Judge Arenda L. Wright Allen's ruling on Feb. 13, 2014, United States District Court For the Eastern District of Virginia (Norfolk Division), 22.

[14] *Murphy v. Ramsey*, 114 U.S. 15, 45 (1885), http://supreme.justia.com/cases/federal/us/114/15/.

[15] Harry V. Jaffa, *A New Birth of Freedom* (Lanham: Rowman and Littlefield Publishers, 2000) 389.

[16] *Baskin v. Bogan*, U.S. Court of Appeals, Seventh Circuit, transcript of Judge Posner's ruling, December 4, 2014.

[17] See: http://www.wsj.com/articles/SB10001424127887323466204578382792759517454; Internet; accessed April 2013.

[18] Ibid.

[19] See: http://www.freedomtomarry.org/blog/c/judicial/www.theseattlelesbian.com/www.theseattlelesbian.com/P640, accessed April, 2013.

[20] Robert Barnes, "Book: Lawyer Who Defended California Gay Marriage Ban Plans Daughter's Gay Wedding," *Washington Post,* April 17, 2014.

[21] Ibid.

[22] Harry V. Jaffa, *Original Intent and the Framers of the Constitution: A Disputed Question* (Washington, DC, 1994), 42.

[23] Quoted at: http://www.washingtonpost.com/blogs/wonkblog/wp/2013/03/26/these-are-the-exchanges-you-need-to-read-from-todays-supreme-court-arguments/; Internet; accessed April, 2013.

[24] See: http://www.nationalreview.com/bench-memos/377111/statement-prop-8-defender-chuck-cooper-ed-whelan; Internet; accessed May 9, 2014.

[25] Heinrich Rommen, *The Natural Law* (Indianapolis: Liberty Fund, 1998), xii.

[26] Gerhart Niemeyer, *The Loss and Recovery of Truth* (South Bend, St. Augustine's Press, 2013), 398.

[27] Francis Cardinal George, O.M.I., "The Wrong Side of History," *Catholic New World*, Oct. 21-Nov. 3, 2012; Internet; accessed April 2, 2015, http://www.catholicnewworld.com/cnwonline/2012/1021/cardinal.aspx.

[28] Cited in Linda C. Raeder, "Voegelin on Gnosticism, Modernity, and the Balance of Consciousness," *Political Science Reviewer*, vol. 36, no. 1: 366.

Cycles, Secularism, and the Prospects for Family Renewal

By Allan C. Carlson

The apparent joint death of faith and family has been argued for at least thirty-five years. Sociologist William D'Antonio, one-time President of the Society for the Scientific Study of Religion, had once maintained that religion and family-life were simply two sides of the same coin: strong faith was correlated with healthy family living. However, in 1980, he concluded that religion and the family had "come to the end of their long affair." The traditional Western family, shaped and reinforced by Christian faith, now ran "counter to the main thrust of American life," specifically individualistic hedonism. Accordingly, what D'Antonio called the religion-family complex could no longer fulfill its task of social control; the present and future belonged to careerism and the private pleasures. He argued that churches should abandon the futile defense of anachronistic dogma. Instead, they should "listen to the people" and "learn from them"—a one-way conversation that would, indeed, lead from a contraceptive mentality and easy abortion to the remarkable concept of same-sex marriage.[1]

Much more recently, Mary Eberstadt asserts in her 2013 book, *How the West Really Lost God: A New Theory of Secularization,* that religious faith declines, or flourishes, in close correlation to family life. Put another way, family decline in Western Europe and North America preceded secularization, and pushed it along. The "religious boom" of the 1940's and 1950's was actually conditioned and encouraged by the "marriage" and "baby" booms of that era. Similarly, it was family decline in the 1960's—driven by equity feminism and the sexual revolution—which drove religious decline, or secularization, symbolized by the infamous cover of *Time* magazine in 1966: "Is God Dead?"[2]

The problem with such pessimistic interpretations is that they lift events of the late 20th century out of a deeper, and much richer, historical context. I am currently working on a book manuscript arguing that there have been four distinct cycles in the history of the family in America. These cycles show periods of a "strengthening" or "weakening" of American family systems around a common normative model, involving: early and nearly universal marriage; high fertility; close attention to parental responsibilities; complementary gender roles; flexible but clear inter-generational bonds; an ideal of family economic autonomy; and—key for us today—religious commitment. Such features have distinguished "the American family" from a "European" model also evident since 1700, involving: late marriage; a high proportion of the adult population "never married"; and lower fertility.[3]

Importantly, these cycles of strength and weakness have occurred in remarkably consistent fifty-year swings. Roughly speaking, periods of strength are evident from 1630 to 1680, from 1730 to 1780, from 1830 to 1880, and from 1930 to 1970: a somewhat shortened cycle of forty years. These "famististic" periods were set off by periods of decline from 1680 to 1730, 1780 to 1830, and 1880 to 1930, with another period of decline—measured statistically—beginning around 1970.

In this paper, I want to focus primarily on the period 1930 to 1970: the most recent "upswing." I will identify some of the *sources* or *causes* of this era of renewal, with a special emphasis on the role played by the Roman Catholics in America in *stimulating* this episode of revival: both *familial* and religious. I will comment only briefly on the era of decline or decay, for its causes and consequences are better known. And I will also consider the prospects for renewal that lie ahead because—if I am correct—a new time of religious and family revival lies in the very near future.

Sources of Family Renewal

I turn your attention, accordingly, to five factors that encouraged family renewal in the 20th century.

First, the foundation of family renewal in mid-20th century America began with political recognition of the family. This story starts with the presidency of Theodore Roosevelt, 1901-1909. He was the first openly pro-life and pro-family president. A student of census numbers, he grew worried as he saw the marriage rate and the birth rate falling in the United States, while the divorce rate climbed. In response, he articulated a family politics that—when judged by Catholic standards—would appear remarkably orthodox.

On birth control, for example, Roosevelt labeled this practice "the capital sin" against civilization, one that meant national death.[4] He thought that the spread of birth control practices during the late 19th century had been due to the power of wrong ideas. He cited "the profound and lasting damage done by Malthus" in his pessimism over population growth "and, to a lesser extent, by John Stuart Mill," in his open advocacy for birth limitation.[5] Roosevelt also blamed the "blatant sham reformers who, in the name of *the new morality*, preach the old, old vice and self-indulgence." These "most foolish of all foolish people who advocate a profoundly immoral attitude toward life" in the name of "reform" through "birth control" were in fact the real problem: the true corrupters of nations.[6]

Roosevelt also blamed the currents of liberal theology found among some American Christians for undermining the child-rich family. In a speech to a group of liberal Protestant theologians, he directly linked the procreation of children to true Americanism:

> If you do not believe in your own [people] enough to wish to see [their numbers] kept up, then you *are not good Americans*, you *are not patriots*; and I for one shall not mourn your extinction; and in such event I shall welcome the advent of a new race that will take your place, because you will have shown that you are not fit to cumber the ground.[7]

Roosevelt also condemned divorce. As he told the National Congress of Mothers in 1905: "Easy divorce is now, as it ever has been, a *bane* to any nation, a *curse* to society, a *menace* to the home, an *incitement* to married unhappiness, and to immorality." Elsewhere, he argued that the "[m]ultiplication of divorces means that there is something rotten in the community, that there is some principle of evil at work."[8]

This president also held a remarkable view of marriage. It should be a full partnership, he said, with "*common* parental care for children, by both father and mother."[9] More broadly, a true marriage would be "a partnership of the soul, the spirit, and the mind, no less than of the body.[10] The "highest ideal" of the family" could be obtained "only where the father and mother stand to each other as lovers and friends."[11]

It's hard to imagine a modern President speaking with such force and eloquence on these subjects. And in truth, even Roosevelt's biographers—including Edmund Morris—mostly ignore these profound insights of the Roughrider. He actually should be remembered as a great champion for *life* and *family*, who charted ways toward domestic revival.

A second source of family renewal grew out of the issue of mass immigration and assimilation into America during the opening decades of the 20th century. In this case, though, the lens is very different: not Hispanics, but *the German-Americans*. In 1900, the German-Americans were the largest group of immigrants in America, and the ones who most worried the older, Anglo-Saxon, Protestant stock. Many German-Americans refused fully to assimilate; they kept their old language; they founded their own parochial schools, Catholic and Lutheran; and they organized into *The Deutsche-Amerikanischer National-Bund*, or The German-American National Alliance. As an advocate for a pluralistic, *multi-cultural* view of America, this *Bund*—which had a special charter from the U.S. Congress—was the *La Raza* of its day. Some eager German-Americans even called for the broad "Germanization" of American life.

The crisis for this community came in 1914-16, as the Great War in Europe heightened ethnic tensions in America. President Woodrow Wilson set out to crush what he called "hyphenated America," with the German-Americans (alongside the anti-English Irish-Americans) as his primary targets. These German-Americans, meanwhile, strove to keep the United States strictly neutral in the war. By early 1917, they had failed, and the institutions of German-Americans were openly, and sometimes violently, suppressed. Even the ratification of the 18th Amendment—prohibiting alcoholic drinks—in early 1919 can be seen as an anti-German act, for all Germans were actually united on only one thing: the importance of beer and wine to a good life.

All the same, the German-Americans had another legacy. Quietly, but with real impact, German-American Christians introduced a new "corporatist worldview" into American life, with a focus on the vital social role played by the intermediary institutions of family, church, and community. Here we see, in historian Jon Gjerde's words, "romantic notions of an organic society composed of people enveloped by groups" taking root in America.[12] Among German Roman Catholics, the influence of this new "Social Catholicism" was particularly strong. In 1891, the German-American Catholic organizations *Central-Verein* and the *Kathiolikentag* passed resolutions praising Pope Leo XIII's new encyclical, *Rerum Novarum*, and pledged to see its principles implemented in the United States. As Father Anton Heiter explained, German-Americans must "enter into the Christian social movement which Leo XIII has so happily inaugurated and to which our Catholic brethren of Germany owe their great success."[13]

German-American authors gave special attention to the qualities and model of the German *hausfrau*—the mother and housewife—as a model for American women. As Albert B. Faust explained in 1911:

> America would not be what it is in vigor, population and the bed-rock civilization [except for] the home training [exemplified] by the German-American housewife. Historically, the emphasis laid upon the household arts, [such] as cooking, sewing, care of the house and children, by so large a formative element of the population from the earliest period of German immigration to the present time, cannot have resulted otherwise than in *impressing the economic advantage of the principle* and furnishing an example for imitation.[14]

These profound images of the traditional Christian German-American home fed into the social politics of the *Maternalist* movement. Sometimes also called Social Feminists, the *Maternalists* worked to reshape American public policy to reinforce the traditional home. Women such as Julia Lathrop, Grace Abbott, Edith Bremer, Frances Kellor, Dr. Josephine Baker, and Mary Anderson argued for a *family wage* for fathers (so that mothers would not have to work.) They also labored to reinforce the *homemaking* role for women, which they saw as an assimilation tool as well: *one motherhood from diversely situated women.*[15]

Between 1912 and 1964, Maternalist ideas dominated the shaping of federal social policy. Early victories included: 1) creation of the U.S. Children's Bureau in 1912, which launched its massive "Baby Saving" campaign, promoted breast feeding, organized National Baby Weeks in 1916 and 1918 involving millions of women, and created Little Mothers Leagues among urban immigrant children; 2) the elevation of Mother's Day by Congress to a National Holiday in 1914; 3) passage of the Smith-Lever and Smith Hughes Acts which provided federal funds for the instruction of girls in home economics; and 4) the Sheppard-Towner Act of 1921, which provided pre- and post-natal care to young mothers and their babies, the first federal medical entitlement.[16]

All of these measures reflected and were—in significant part—the result of distinctive German-American views of motherhood, family, and home. While the nativists of the early 20th century had suppressed the more visible cultural attributes of the German-American, these deeper family-centered sentiments remained and helped to shape a family-centered interlude after 1930. Perhaps America was "Germanized" after all; if so, this was to the special benefit of families, mothers, and babies.

A third source of family renewal was, accordingly, public policy; specifically—and perhaps surprisingly—the New Deal of the 1930's, which in terms of social policy was a continuation of the Maternalist campaign. Here, it is useful to note that contemporary feminist historians hate, even loathe, the New Deal. Recent histories covering the 1930's by feminist authors uniformly condemn the social policies of Franklin D. Roosevelt.[17] Why? For the simple, but usually unappreciated, fact that virtually every New Deal policy initiative assumed the importance and structure of the traditional family: a breadwinning father earning a "family wage"; a homemaking mother committed to the care of children; and an *autonomous home* cast as the centerpiece of American society. The New Deal Maternalists, for example, were *strict foes* of *daycare*, believing that children should be raised by their mothers in the home.

Key architects of the New Deal also carried Catholic ideals into the system. For example, Msgr. John Ryan—professor of social ethics at The Catholic University of America and America's foremost advocate of a "family wage" for fathers—served on the panel that created the Social Security Act of 1935. Arthur Altmeyer, a German-American Catholic from Wisconsin, was the chief architect of the Social Security Amendments of 1939. This important measure introduced the extra pension for homemakers, worth 50 percent of their husbands' benefits, and it created survivors' benefits for women and children. This measure made support of marriage, the "family wage," the stay-at-home mother, and the large family the favored objects of American public policy. Deviations from these norms—divorce, illegitimacy, working mothers, deliberate childlessness—faced significant financial disincentives. The whole New Deal project was ably summed up by Molly Dewson, head of women's activities for the Democratic Party:

> [W]hen you begin to help the family to attain some security you are at the same time beginning to erect a National structure for the same purpose. *Through the well-being of the family*, we create the well-being of The Nation.[18]

In short, the New Deal used the state to reinforce the family in a very traditional form. This is one reason why so many active Catholics during the 1930's, 1940's, and 1950's voted Democratic—it was the *party of the family*.

Fourth, this episode of family renewal also enjoyed the encouragement of the popular media. Representative here are the work and goals of Henry Luce, founder and editor of *Time, Life* and *Fortune* magazines. *Life* magazine, in particular, showed an enormous influence by the late 1940's: *one-third* of all American families were subscribers to this weekly. Luce *consciously* used this magazine to promote an American identity rooted in images of family and faith, to bind the nation together as the heir and protector of Western civilization. As he wrote in one planning memo:

> The great significance of *Life* is that it includes among its readers all manners and kinds of Americans....*Life* is for highbrows and low-brows, for women and for men and even for children, for old and young, for Easterners and Westerners, for "rich" and "poor" in the American sense. This could only happen in America—and only in [the] mid-twentieth century. It could *only happen with pictures*....Here is the society bound together in broad and deep consensus yet not a conformist society.[19]

On religious questions, a major issue for Luce was the place of Catholicism in America. *Life* magazine regularly featured Catholic themes and personalities, such as the Jesuit scholar John Courtney Murray. This is usually attributed to the influence of Luce's wife, Clare Boothe Luce, one of the most famous Catholic converts of the 1940's. Indeed, when the managing editor of *Life*, Joseph Thorndike, resigned in 1948, he privately confided to his successor that he worried about the Catholic Church taking over the magazine.[20] Yet it seems clear that Luce's public celebration of Catholicism had deeper purposes. Luce, a Presbyterian, recognized that America could not be *unified* and *active* in the world without the loyalty of its largest single religious denomination. Catholicism and America must be reconciled, for the good of the nation. This was a central part of Henry Luce's project.

Fifth, lay Catholic activism formed still another component of family renewal in mid-century America. Symbolic of this was the creation of La Leche League in the 1950's. All seven founders of the League were Roman Catholic women from the Chicago area. They had begun to meet as an action cell of the Christian Family Movement. Using a format designed by Canon Joseph Cardijn, the women met to discuss theology and social action, with concern not just for "the betterment of their own family situations but also with the life of families everywhere." As young mothers, these women soon grafted onto their conversations a common interest in natural childbirth and breastfeeding. Seeking a name for their new entity, they responded favorably to a suggestion by one of their husbands, an obstetrician, who commonly gave to his pregnant patients medals from a St. Augustine, Florida, shrine, dedicated to the Madonna: Nuestra Señora de *La Leche* y Buen Parto ("Our Lady of Happy Delivery and Plentiful Milk").[21]

So constituted, La Leche League—in the words of historian Lynn Weiner—"arose to defend traditional domesticity against the assaults of modern industrial life and to dignify the physical, biological side of motherhood in ways that proved to have surprising appeal to many Americans." Where 19th-century notions of "true womanhood" had focused on piety and moral purity, La Leche League stressed naturalism: mother and baby as symbols of simplicity and nature. In this way, the League reinvigorated the earlier Maternalist campaign with new language and activism, focused on "the womanly art of breastfeeding." Thousands of League groups mushroomed across the land.[22]

The "Baby Boom" and Catholicism

Indeed, the 1930-1970 era produced an extraordinary, almost "heroic," flowering of Catholic family life in America. Although fertility rose for all American religious groups during this period, it rose far more rapidly and continued longer among Catholics. There were signs that the celebrated American "baby boom" was largely a Catholic phenomenon. The total marital fertility rate for non-Catholics averaged 3.15 children per woman in 1951-55 and 3.14 in 1961-65; for Catholics, the respective figures were 3.54 and 4.25. More dramatic was the return of the large Catholic family: in a survey conducted in 1952-55, only 10 percent of Catholics under age 40 reported having four or more children, a figure close to the 9 percent for Protestants. By 1957-59, the Protestant figure was unchanged, but the proportion for Catholics had shot up to 22 percent.

Still more surprising was the nature of this resurgence in Catholic fertility. It flourished among the best educated: Catholic women who had attended college were bearing more children than Catholic women without a high school diploma. Increased fertility was also found primarily among younger parents: through 1965, each new cohort of parents was more pro-natalist in its attitudes than the group before. And it had a clear religious focus: more frequent attendance at Mass was related to more births. In addition, the rise in fertility was part of a broader commitment to family life: surveys repeatedly showed Catholic extended-family bonds to be more durable and enjoyment of the parenting task more intense than among non-Catholics. Indeed, the Catholic family ethic, resting on devotion to Church teachings, seemed to be reaching new highs in the mid-1960s. Among the American laity, at least, there was no crisis of faith.[23]

Within ten years, though, all of these qualities appeared to have collapsed, utterly and completely, prompting a spate of articles on "the end of Catholic fertility." There is little doubt that the currents of ideas affecting Catholicism in the late 1960s—challenges to traditional practices and hierarchical authority in the wake of Vatican II, the seeming papal encouragement of debate on the contraceptive question in the mid-1960s (followed by the stunning reaffirmation of orthodoxy in 1968 in *Humanae Vitae*), and the impact of feminist and neo-Malthusian tenets on key Catholic elites—lay partly behind this shift. Dissent became legitimized, and doctrinal uncertainty grew. Given the new divisions among theologians and Church leaders, it appears that a significant portion of the laity may simply have followed the easiest of several disputed paths of obedience.[24]

Indeed, changes in lay Catholic attitudes and behavior concerning the family have been traced to the specific years 1967-71. In their detailed study of Catholic fertility in Rhode Island, Leon Bouvier and S.L.N. Rao found that average expected family size among Catholics fell from 3.3 children to 2.8 in that short four-year period, a substantially greater decline than seen among Protestants. This fall in expected fertility was sharpest for the better educated: among Catholic women with some college education, the decline was from 3.7 to 2.7 children. Moreover, frequency of attendance at Mass no longer proved to be related to fertility. Even the large family ideal vanished: as late as 1967, 28 percent of "devout" Catholics planned to have five or more children; by 1971, less than 7 percent did.[25]

The Post-Post-Modern Family?

What, then, are the prospects for a new cycle of family renewal? If my historical theory holds true, then we should expect to see evidence of renewal within the next five years.

In this light, Eric Kaufmann's 2012 book, *Shall the Religious Inherit the Earth?*, offers a provocative look at the human future. A political scientist at University of London and a self-identified secular liberal, Kaufmann nonetheless boldly concludes, "Religious fundamentalists are on course to take over the world through demography." (He uses the old American Protestant term "fundamentalists" here broadly to describe Jews, Christians, and Muslims worldwide who take their beliefs seriously enough to allow scriptural teachings on marriage and procreation to influence their behavior.) The future of the human race, he argues, lies with groups such as American Mormons, Old-Order Anabaptists, Haredi Jews, Salafi Islamists, Quiverfull Protestants, and "Laestadian Lutherans" (a sect found in the north woods of Finland and Sweden). These are religious communions still faithful to God's command, "Be fruitful and multiply." With fertility otherwise tumbling around the globe, these religious groups—with total fertility rates of between four and eight births per woman—are already expanding their relative share of the population. Compounded over four generations, the transition would prove staggering.[26]

Kaufmann skillfully dismantles the modern liberal myth that secularism is on the march and will dominate the future. Instead, he argues, "We have embarked on a particularly turbulent phase of history in which the frailty of secular liberalism will become ever more apparent." At the same time, Kaufmann explains how the liberal values of tolerance and pluralism suck the life out of "moderate" religion, while allowing fundamentalist subcultures to emerge and grow. As he summarizes, "Secularism, like DDT, wiped out much of its opposition but also gave rise to new, resistant strains of religion."

Kaufmann gives extensive attention to several "Enlightenment-resistant" groups: the ultra-orthodox Haredi, who will shortly constitute the majority of all people in Israel displacing the low-fertility secular Jews who founded the country; the American Mormons, who are still increasing at a rate of 40 percent per decade; the "Quiverfull" Evangelicals, who reject the use of birth control; and the Old-Order Amish, who have expanded from 5,000 adherents in 1900 to more than 300,000 today. While "seculars" increasingly avoid marriage and children, these faith communities have rediscovered the biblical injunction to reproduce and have "thrived in the most individualistic, profane, Western societies."

Curiously, Kaufmann gives little attention to signs of the same phenomenon within Roman Catholicism. It is clear, though, that pockets of high fertility can also be found in American "Latin Mass" congregations and other traditional settings. They are aspects of the same development.

The political effects of these changes, Kaufmann predicts, will be huge. Due to differential fertility between "seculars" and "fundamentalists," by 2100 "three-quarters of America may be pro-life. Their activism will leap over the borders of the 'Redeemer Nation' to evangelize the world." Kaufmann's closing words should instill fear in every secular pagan mind:

> It will be a century or more before the world completes its demographic transition. There is still too much smoke in the air for us to pick out the peaks and valleys of the emerging social order. This much seems certain: without [a new secular] ideology to inspire social cohesion, fundamentalism cannot be stopped. The religious shall inherit the earth.[27]

Might I add, "May it be so"?

Notes

[1] William V. D'Antonio, "The Family and Religion: Exploring a Changing Relationship," *Journal for the Scientific Study of Religion* 19 (June 1980), 89-104; and William V. D'Antonio and Joan Aldous, *Families and Religions: Conflict and Change in Modern Society* (Beverley Hills: SAGE Publications, 1983), 10-14, 81-106.

[2] See: Mary Eberstadt, *How the West Really Lost God: A New Theory of Secularization* (West Conshohocken, PA: Templeton Press, 2013).

[3] J. Hajnal, "European Marriage Patterns in Perspective," in D.V. Glass and D.E.C. Eversley, *Population in History: Essays in Historical Demography* (London: Edward Arnold, 1965), 101-106.

[4] Theodore Roosevelt, *The Foes of Our Own Household* (New York: George H. Dorân, 1917), 250-51.

[5] Theodore Roosevelt, *The Works of Theodore Roosevelt—Memorial Edition, Vol. XIV* (New York: Charles Scribner's Sons, 1924), 151-52, 163 165.

[6] Roosevelt, *Foes of Our Own Household*, 250-51.

[7] Theodore Roosevelt, *Realizable Ideals: The Earl Lectures* [1911], in Roosevelt, *Works, XXII*, 600.

[8] Roosevelt, *Works, XVIII*, 231; *XXII*, 594.

[9] Roosevelt, *Works, XVIII*, 284.

[10] Roosevelt, *Foes of Our Own Household*, 239.

[11] John A. Lester, ed., *The Americanism of Theodore Roosevelt* (Boston: Houghton Mifflin, 1923), 69.

[12] Jon Gjerde, *The Minds of the West: Ethnocultural Evolution in the Rural Middle West, 1830-1917* (Chapel Hill: University of North Caroline Press, 1997), 252, 261.

[13] Philip Gleason, *The Conservative Reformers: German-American Catholics and the Social Order* (Notre Dame, IN: University of Notre Dame Press, 1968), 69-83.

[14] Albert Bernhardt Faust, *The German Element in the United States, Vol. II* (Boston: Houghton Mifflin, 1909), 463.

[15] See: Cora Winchell, "Homemaking as a Phase of Citizenship," *The Journal of Home Economics* 14 (January 1922), 30, 32-33.

[16] Molly Ladd-Taylor, "My Work Came Out of Agony and Grief: Mothers and the Making of the Sheppard-Towner Act," in Seth Koven and Sonja Michel, eds., *Mothers of a New World: Maternalist Politics and the Origins of the Welfare State* New York: Routledge, 1993), 324.

[17] For example, see: Gwendolyn Mink, *The Wages of Motherhood: Inequality in the Welfare State, 1917-1942* (Ithaca, NY: Cornell University Press, 1995), 171; and Alice Kessler-Harris, *Out to Work: A History of Wage-Earning Women in the United States* (New York: Oxford University Press, 1982), 251.

[18] Quoted in: Alice Kessler-Harris, "Designing Women and Old Fools: The Construction of the Social Security Amendments of 1939," in Linda Kerber, Alice Kessler-Harris, and Kathryn Kish Sklar, eds., *U.S. History as Women's History* (Chapel Hill: University of North Carolina Press, 1995), 87. Emphasis in the original.

[19] Memorandum ["Confidential and Restricted"], Henry Luce to Mr. Larsen, 6 December 1956, Time, Inc. Archives, New York.

[20] Interview by the author with Edward Thompson, 11 December 1984, Hudson, New York.

[21] Lynn Y. Weiner, "Reconstructing Motherhood: The La Leche League in Postwar America," *The Journal of American History* 80 (March 1994), 1360.

[22] Weiner, "Reconstructing Motherhood," 1358.

[23] See William D. Mosher, David P. Johnson, and Marjorie C. Horn, "Religion and Fertility in the United States: The Importance of Marriage Patterns and Hispanic Origin," *Demography* 23 (Aug. 1986): 367-69; Lincoln H. Day, "Natality and Ethnocentrism: Some Relationships Suggested by an Analysis of Catholic-Protestant Differentials," *Population Studies* 22 (1968): 27-30; and Gerhard Lenski, *The Religious Factor: A Sociologist's Inquiry* (New York: Doubleday, 1961), 203, 215-18.

[24] See Charles F. Westoff and Elise T. Jones, "The End of 'Catholic' Fertility," *Demography* 16 (May 1979), 209-11; Gerhard Lenski, "The Religious Factor in Detroit:

Revisited," *American Sociological Review* 36 (1971), 48-50; Mary Daly, "After the Death of God the Father: Women's Liberation and the Transformation of Christian Consciousness," *Commonweal* (Mar. 12, 1971), reprinted in Carol P. Christ and Judith Plaskow, eds., *Womanspirit Rising* (New York: Harper & Row, 1976), 53-62; and *Humanae Vitae*, trans. M.A. Caligari (Cincinnati, OH: Couple to Couple League, 1983).

[25] Leon Bouvier and S.L.N. Rao, *Socio-religious Factors in Fertility Decline* (Cambridge, MA: Ballinger, 1975), 1-4, 84-91, 156, 158; Charles F. Westoff and Larry Bumpass, "The Revolution in Birth Control Practices of U.S. Roman Catholics," *Science* 1979 (Jan. 12, 1973): 41-44; Andrew Greeley, *The American Catholic: A Social Portrait* (New York: Basic Books, 1977), 189; and Charles F. Westoff and Elise T. Jones, "The Secularization of U.S. Catholic Birth Control Practices," *Family Planning Perspectives* 9 (Sept.-Oct. 1977): 203-7.

[26] Eric Kaufmann, *Shall the Religious Inherit the Earth? Demography and Politics in the Twenty-First Century* (London: Profile Books, 2012).

[27] Kaufmann, *Shall the Religious Inherit the Earth?*, 269.

Media Matter: Shaping Public Opinion for the Gospel

By Sheila Liaugminas

In the beginning was the Word, and the Word was with God, and the Word was God. (John 1:1)

Why did it all begin with the Word?

One Bible commentary tries to help us grasp this all important idea by explaining that in the one, singular, unique, eternal Word, God *expresses* His entire essence. Thus, the prologue of the Gospel of John elevates expression to the divine. John declares that this most perfect divine expression broke through eternity into time to communicate all truth about life. John calls the Word "the true light that enlightens every man," but St. John Chrysostom asked, in a homily: "If he enlightens every man who comes into the world, how is it that so many have remained unenlightened?" He answers his rhetorical question by noting that some people "deliberately close the eyes of their minds," and "do not wish to receive the beams of this light." And thus it has been, from the beginning.

However, we have the same mandate the Apostles did to spread the light of truth of human life and dignity. Unlike them, we have the means to reach the whole world through modern communications media, in its various means and rapidly advancing technologies, making the global village even smaller and its citizens ever closer. But only in some respects. If they are reachable at all, it will take prudent care and considerable effort to attract their attention with the true, good, and beautiful.

The theme of this book and the conference that brought it forth, "Challenging the Secular Culture: A Call to Christians," is both daring and daunting, ennobling and enervating. We have to be daring and ennobling, we who stand even here with something to say to and about the secular culture, and call on and call out our fellow Christians to take up the challenge and opportunity the crisis of culture presents. It is for us to show the world another way, as it ever has been for Christians.

I propose to approach my topic as one who journeys with a map, starting with the purpose of the venture and effort first, then taking stock of the landscape and setting at the particular moment of scrutiny and discernment, and then finally and determinedly, mapping out where to go to reach a desired destination, or at least advance in that direction.

The purpose in doing this book and the conference it was based on is the Church's purpose, through different pontificates and over many decades, in issuing messages on communications media, declaring a World Day of Communication each year and delivering a papal address for that, holding Vatican conferences and even the first-ever "blogger meet-up," as the bloggers who attended dubbed it, to give credence and respect to their considerable presence and influence on the global network we know as the Internet.

Going back to Vatican II, in 1963 the Council issued *Inter Mirifica,* the *Decree on the Means of Social Communications*, under Pope Paul VI, who a dozen years later wrote *Evangelii Nuntiandi* (*On Evangelization in the Modern World*) in which he said, "Modern man listens more willingly to witnesses than to teachers, and if he does listen to teachers, it is because they are witnesses." Pope John Paul II addressed this prolifically, saying "communications is a moral act." His Apostolic Letter *Rapid Development*, his last major document, is not only my mission statement but serves that purpose for some of my colleagues either in Catholic media, or Catholics in secular media. It addressed the importance of the media in advancing the truth about humanity and human dignity and life, and continuing the mission of the Church. Pope Benedict XVI wrote incisively and eloquently about the digital universe, calling on people not to shun it but to humanize it. Pope Francis called the Internet a "gift from God" in his 2014 World Day of Communications Message: "Communication at the Service of an Authentic Culture of Encounter."

This has been and remains an important pursuit and focus in the life of the Church, "going out to all the world to tell the good news," by all means possible. St. Paul believed he had reached the known world in his time, and he very nearly had. The extent to which the ability to reach the known world in this time has become simple for us all defies an apt description. It is time to engage the new *areopagus*.

The Arena of Ideas and Modern Media

Catholic historian Christopher Dawson was certainly one of the greatest students and teachers of the powerful role the relationship between religion and culture has on civilization. He saw the Incarnation as the "hinge event" that altered human history and transformed human nature, revealing our dignity to ourselves and with that, the new and elevated principles that must guide a civilization of people with such an ennobled identity.

An important function of civilization is, of course, communication—in the form of storytelling, cultural "narrative," or any means of the expression of truth in the spoken or written word that determines relationships and informs life in community. When we hear ideas about ourselves that reflect a distorted view of what we believe to be our true image, in the Christian understanding of human anthropology and common life, we either lose trust in the messenger, or accept an altered message and let it change our thinking.

It's amazing how often history repeats itself, including and especially the errors we somehow didn't learn to avoid

Dawson saw the errors of his early twentieth century age as a repeat of those in the ages of Augustine and Ignatius of Loyola. Both of those ages recognized neither moral laws nor human rights. We are there yet again, and Dawson's prism is particularly important to apply now.

He warned about the revolt against Christian moral teachings and especially against giving importance to individual conscience. Dawson was well aware of the role communication media played in forming consciences, writing in his 1935 book *Religion and the Modern State* that "the State…will more and more tend to control public opinion in general by its organs of instruction and propaganda….The whole tendency of modern civilization is, in fact, to concentrate the control of opinion in a few hands."

That was almost three decades after the Society of Professional Journalists (SPJ) was established. Dawson was writing prolifically about morality and culture, and their importance in an age of increased travel and communication. And when he wrote that book, he was seeing and warning of nations in which the control of opinion drifted into the hands of a relatively few. And yet, interestingly, the SPJ had a code of ethics then, which can still be found on its current website. It seems to be the epitome of self-governing, autonomous service of information about the people to the people, answerable to no State. The Preamble stated that:

> Members of the Society of Professional Journalists believe that public enlightenment is the forerunner of justice and the foundation of democracy. Ethical journalism strives to ensure the free exchange of information that is accurate, fair and thorough. An ethical journalist acts with integrity.

On what does an organization base a set of ethical guidelines, especially one so formative for public opinion and individual consciences as the press? How did the Society define justice, ethical journalism, fairness and integrity?

The code was revised as recently as 2014, and it appears on the Society's website. Following my oft-repeated advice to "presume good intentions," I will not ask some obvious questions about how well these ethics are applied, accessed, or even known by today's journalists or people who work in media.

News outlets have downsized their staffs and re-envisioned their purpose and mission and operations, so it's a new day and if any rules apply, they tend to be new ones. But they have retained some or much of their former clout. Though the "mainstream" media have polled lower and lower in public approval ratings, they are still powerful and important in the formation of our minds, thoughts, and ideas. We should not underestimate that. We should engage it. What gives media so much influence?

The Power of Words

Citizens have long turned to the media to get information about events in the news, not knowing the process of selection those news stories went through before making it to the pages or screens of media outlets. Famous journalist, political theorist and once government propagandist Walter Lippman filled his famous book *Public Opinion* with startlingly simple analyses and anecdotes of the relationship between people and the press they follow to learn what's happening in the world. Somewhere around the middle of the book, in the middle of a paragraph and mid-sentence, he said this: "...most information when it reaches us carries with it an aura of suggestion as to how we ought to feel about the news." And that was in the early 20th century.

As most of us know, news stories are—to varying degrees—shaped, manipulated and crafted to elicit or trigger a certain instinctive response in your mind and emotions. It has been called "semantic engineering" in more recent times.

In *Abuse of Language, Abuse of Power*, Joseph Pieper called it the "corruption of the word," which he traced back to Plato's lifelong battle with the sophists, "those highly paid and popularly applauded experts in the art of twisting words, who were able to sweet-talk something bad into something good and to turn white into black."

He goes on: "The specific threat, for Plato, comes from the sophists' way of cultivating the word with exceptional awareness of linguistic nuances...perfecting the employment of verbal construction to crafty limits, thereby—and precisely in this—corrupting the meaning and the dignity of the very same words."

This is important to understand, today.

So highly did Pieper, and Plato whom he cites, regard truth and its expression, Pieper said, "*...word and language form the medium that sustains the common existence of the human spirit as such*" (emphasis added).

Today's influential culture-shapers in the media, both news and entertainment media, do not reflect awareness or acceptance of the common existence of the human spirit, nor a Christian understanding of the human spirit, nor even the sense or existence of the transcendent.

Common vocabulary has been altered to create new perceptions and, as we know, perception becomes reality. Almost anything can be justified by redefining words and crafting them into messages favorable to actions or behaviors people otherwise would not accept. Then, they're presented authoritatively and repeated often by other authorities, in news media, politics, social media, entertainment media, and in a short time, cultural trends are not only established, but they gain currency in public opinion.

Read or re-read Aldous Huxley's *Brave New World* and George Orwell's *1984*. Considering where we are with abortion, harvesting fetal body parts, genetic engineering, stem cell research, cloning, euthanasia, assisted suicide, mass deception and thought control, Huxley and Orwell were prophetic in their accounts of a captive, clueless, and endangered society.

How did it become legal to kill babies? The re-writing of the Constitution that was required to do this probably stands as one of the most sweeping abuses of the control of language since Hitler's re-crafting of words to justify genocide by calling Jews "parasites," robbing them of their human dignity in terrible ways. The *Dred Scott* decision declared that slaves did not have personhood, thus no Constitutional rights. *Roe v. Wade* declared that although an unborn baby may have a heart and a brain and is biologically human, he or she is not a person, and thus has no constitutional rights.

"The battle to restore protection to our pre-born brothers and sisters is in many ways a war of words," said the director of Priests for Life. Since there is no rational defense for killing babies, leaders of the abortion movement resorted to thought control, or propaganda. The groundwork was prepared decades ago.

"Semantic Gymnastics"

The now infamous September 1970 editorial in *California Medicine*, the journal of the California Medical Association, is emblematic of a cultural turning point in delivering, and accepting, a once unacceptable message.

The CMA acknowledged the traditional Judeo-Christian ethic of our country, which placed intrinsic value on every human life at all stages. It recognized that this ethic has been held sacred in the Judeo-Christian heritage, informing most laws and social policies. But then the editorial argued that a population explosion compounded by the "quality of life" issue, combined with "unprecedented technologic progress and achievement," have all together posed "new facts and social realities," ones the CMA believed were "within the power of humans to control."

Therefore, the editorial proposed this:

> It will become necessary and acceptable to place relative rather than absolute values on such things as human lives... Since the old ethic has not yet been fully displaced it has been necessary to separate the idea of abortion from the idea of killing, which continues to be socially abhorrent. The result has been a curious avoidance of the scientific fact, which everyone really knows, that human life begins at conception and is continuous whether intra-or extra-uterine until death. The very considerable semantic gymnastics which are required to rationalize abortion as anything but taking a human life

> would be ludicrous if they were not often put forth under socially impeccable auspices. It is suggested that this schizophrenic sort of subterfuge is necessary because while a new ethic is being accepted the old one has not yet been rejected.

The editorial went on to anticipate "birth control and birth selection [extending] inevitably to death selection and death control whether by the individual or by society, [causing] public and professional determinations of when and when not to use scarce resources."

And it concluded: "It is not too early for our profession to examine this new ethic...and prepare to apply it in a rational development for the fulfillment and betterment of mankind in what is almost certain to be a biologically oriented world society."

How did this become a landmark for cultural acceptance of what had been considered by that culture as immoral and inhumane? To repeat, it's amazing how often history repeats itself, including and especially the errors we somehow didn't learn to avoid. In Dr. Dietrich von Hildebrand's memoir, *My Battle Against Hitler: Faith, Truth and Defiance in the Shadow of the Third Reich* (which was translated, edited and published by the Hildebrand Legacy Project, based at Franciscan University of Steubenville), we read the following:

> Every form of anti-personalism (which is seen most clearly in Bolshevism and National Socialism) is a logical consequence of liberalism's failure to recognize the true essence and value of the person. But such anti-personalism goes far beyond what existed in liberalism, since it intensifies the individualistic error and disvalue. Anti-personalism is the great and terrible danger of our times. Irrespective of the guise under which it presents itself, this poison must not be allowed a role in the construction of genuine community.

In a visit with von Hildebrand's wife, Dr. Alice von Hildebrand, in January 2015 at her New York home, in an engaging conversation, I opened my copy of the book to that flagged page and repeated these words and expressed my amazement that we have not learned from the errors of history and seem to be in that dangerous situation again today. She said, "No! It's worse now!" And she stated what should be obvious: that today these dangers to genuine personalism and human dignity are many and they are not posed by uniformed jackboots, but disguised in countless ways and posed by other Americans, in media and politics especially, as social policies and laws that serve the common good and advance human "rights" and "freedom" and "social justice," among other slogans.

Pope John Paul II frequently, throughout his life and pontificate, talked about such rights and wrongs, and spoke out for human dignity and the true understanding of personalism, and called distortions of it "skepticism regarding the very existence of moral truth and an objective moral law" in contemporary society. That certainly describes our society.

In an *ad limina* address to bishops in America, in 1998, Pope John Paul said, "This attitude is quite prevalent in the cultural institutions that influence public opinion, and, it must be said, is commonplace in many of your country's academic, political and legal structures." And, we can add, in the powerful mainstream media.

In that address, John Paul connected this disorder with the misunderstanding and misuse of conscience, free will, and freedom:

> Culturally powerful forces insist that the rights of conscience are violated by the very idea that there exists a moral law ascribed in our humanity, which we can come to know by reflecting on our nature and our actions, and which lays certain obligations upon us because we recognize them as universally true and binding....Conscience is that inner place where "man detects a law which he does not impose upon himself, but which holds him to obedience" (*Gaudium et Spes* #16)
>
> Freedom of conscience is never freedom from the truth but always and only freedom in the truth....When the Church teaches, for example, that abortion, sterilization or euthanasia are always morally inadmissible, she is giving expression to the universal moral law inscribed on the human heart, and is therefore teaching something which is binding on everyone's conscience....A society or culture which wishes to survive cannot declare the spiritual dimension of the human person to be irrelevant to public life.

And yet, that's exactly what big media and big politics have been doing, and especially now when the free exercise of religion became a culture battle escalated to new heights.

Pope Benedict, time and again, said virtually those same words of John Paul, and both popes said them to the UN General Assembly in their addresses to that august body. The spiritual dimension of the human person is pre-eminent and must be respected as our "first freedom."

In January 2012, Pope Benedict warned the Church in the US that "radical secularism" was posing new threats to religious liberty in this country. It was key timing, just after the *Hosanna Tabor* Supreme Court case in which thejustices unanimously upheld religious freedom rights, and Benedict's message was just before the HHS mandate was issued. He said:

> At the heart of every culture, whether perceived or not, is a consensus about the nature of reality and the moral good, and thus about the conditions for human flourishing. In America, that consensus, as enshrined in your nation's founding

> documents, was grounded in a worldview shaped not only by faith but a commitment to certain ethical principles deriving from nature and nature's God. Today that consensus has eroded significantly in the face of powerful new cultural currents which are not only directly opposed to core moral teachings of the Judeo-Christian tradition, but increasingly hostile to Christianity as such....

Our nation's opinion shapers in politics and media especially are driving those powerful cultural currents. Pope Benedict continued:

> The Church's defense of a moral reasoning based on the natural law is grounded on her conviction that this law is not a threat to our freedom, but rather a "language" which enables us to understand ourselves and the truth of our being, and so to shape a more just and humane world....

That is a key statement in all times, but it has become increasingly pressing in recent years since the federal HHS mandate was issued, violating the faith and conscience of whole populations of Americans. And even more pressing in recent weeks since states have passed religious freedom laws virtually identical to the federal one widely accepted since 1993, but now denounced and refuted, with lies and distortions, claiming that they permit and protect discrimination. They do not. But in the haste to fix these laws and quell the fury of the law's opponents, the "fix" no longer gave people of faith who live according to their morally informed beliefs protection from those who would discriminate against *them.*

Nation, we have a problem.

If it sounds like some of the same warnings, reports, and observations have been repeated in this paper, it's because they have. Over and over, from scholars and authors, clergy and popes, from Plato to Pieper to Pope Francis.

Moral Confusion

Walter Lippman wrote *Public Opinion* after seeing how newspaper reports on the Russian Revolution were distorted and inaccurate, based not on facts but the hopes of those doing the reporting. His fundamental concern then is ours today, access to accurate information. He argued that unbiased information was essential because "decisions in a modern state tend to be made by the interaction, not of Congress and the executive, but of public opinion and the executive."

It's amazing that he didn't write those words in our time.

When media are complicit in advancing false narratives about news events, and social media users launch campaigns to advance those false narratives, the falsehoods take on a life of their own and people are persuaded.

Words are used as tools and weapons. Consider the effect of using positive words like "pro" and "choice," "freedom" and "rights" to describe an agenda like abortion on demand, while pro-life advocates for human rights and dignity are called "anti-abortion," "anti-choice" etc. So "choice" covers abortion, "compassion" is now the mantle for euthanasia, and "equality" the mantle that covers the movement to redefine marriage in law.

Consider this statement from Joseph Pieper about distortion of language and its power:

> [T]he place of authentic reality is taken over by a fictitious reality; my perception is indeed still directed toward an object, but now it is a pseudo-reality, deceptively appearing as being real, so much so that it becomes almost impossible anymore to discern the truth....For the general public is being reduced to a state where people not only are unable to find out about the truth but also become unable even to search for the truth because they are satisfied with deception and trickery that have determined their convictions, satisfied with a fictitious reality created by design through the abuse of language.

We need bold and unambiguous language.

Cardinal Francis George, in a column in the Chicago Archdiocesan newspaper *The Catholic New World* (October 25, 1998), wrote:

> [P]olitical questions which influence our nation's policies on respect for life and its preservation from conception to natural death are the defining issues before us. This is not a narrow or "single issue" approach. Was slavery a "single issue"? Is the economy a "single issue"? Respect for life is no more a single issue than is concern for freedom....We will need personal holiness to rebuild a moral society on a foundation of objective truth.

Do Something

Consider yourself encouraged. How are we doing with personal holiness, for starters? And personal witness of our belief in the true, the good, and the beautiful? And countering false claims with clarity? We get galvanized over the threat of losing our right to express Catholic faith, Christian beliefs, and Gospel values in public, and to remain free to let our convictions inform our decisions and actions.

But here's a challenging question: how well have we stood up for our beliefs until this threat to our religious freedom escalated in 2012? We tend to appreciate what we had after we've lost it, and we find ourselves imagining the real loss of this freedom for the first time. The abortion movement got years ahead of us before the pro-life movement gained ground and so much so, we're now ahead of a diminished abortion industry, though they remain powerful with political allies, and the considerable power of elite media.

But consider what I call the "power of one." Watch a video of Live Action's Lila Rose debating abortion advocates on cable news networks (I can think of the one on CNN's Crossfire with NARAL's Ilyse Hogue, or on Fox News with Tamara Holder) or Lila in March 2015 at the United Nations in a packed auditorium during the UN Commission on the Status of Women conference, defending women, children and human dignity, with rousing applause and the gratitude of the Permanent Observer to the Holy See.

Watch a video of Heritage Foundation Fellow Ryan T. Anderson on any number of news shows speaking from facts and reason about marriage law or religious liberty—calmly, clearly, and charitably—and getting the ire of CNN's Piers Morgan or Don Lemon, or MSNBC's Ed Schultz. These are two young adults making a huge difference and inspiring huge followings by speaking out in whatever media is available to them, or using media available to all of us.

Back when abortionist Kermit Gosnell was finally stopped by authorities from committing atrocities in what those authorities dubbed a "house of horrors," a Pennsylvania abortion clinic that had to be inspected by jurors in Hazmat suits to prepare for his trial, it was horrific and finally a graphic, landmark case of the "logic of abortion" carried through to its conclusion. But even then, the trial began with an empty media section—until pro-life leader Bryan Kemper rallied some fellow pro-life leaders to launch a well-coordinated Twitter campaign calling on media to cover the trial. It worked, and those seats were filled and the story got out in big media, finally. It seemed the abortion industry would never recover from the powerful fallout of that revelation.

But how quickly the story went away.

In a sort of reverse case, the *Rolling Stone* magazine cover story of an alleged rape case at the University of Virginia that caused widespread coverage filling news cycles across nearly all major media turned out to be a complete hoax. The coverage went away, except for a few outlets.

If one is familiar with Jean Baudrillard, it is either because the person is a scholar, a student of extensive research, or a fan of *The Matrix*, which showed Neo opening his copy of Baudrillard's book *Simulacra and Simulation* in a now famous scene. One of Baudrillard's best known media theories was of what he called the "non-event," or media's manipulation of story and symbol, and therefore public perception of it, or lack thereof.

The entertainment media are using popular culture and the film industry to advance the euthanasia movement's cause and influence public opinion about assisted suicide as the way to insure the "right to die" at the time and by the means of one's choosing. Dawson already saw the power of this and other media when he wrote *Religion and the Modern State*:

> As our civilization becomes more completely mechanized it becomes easier to control, and the organs of control become more centralized. It is true that these things are not usually regarded as having much relevance to the religious issue. But

> we may ask ourselves—do people go to the cinema or to church? Does not the cinema take the place that was formerly occupied by church and chapel? Has not Hollywood got a distinct ethic of its own which influences the minds of its audiences? Is this ethic in any sense Christian?

Film industry insider and faithful Catholic Barbara Nicolosi says that Hollywood, "for over a century, the undisputed engine of global storytelling…is now in a crisis." She says:

> By removing suffering and the meaning of suffering from our culture, we make the final step in denying and defying our creature-hood….We need an emotionally winning language for this fight. If we lose the fight on euthanasia, we lose our souls….We must be aggressive in exposing the deceptions driving the euthanasia movement—lies like the implication that personhood can somehow disappear from a wounded human body. Or that a human life could ever lose its value. Or that suicide can be a courageous act. We must contradict the notion that suffering is the worst thing that can happen to a person.

And do it by all means. We have so many available to us today, from the spoken word to the proliferation of ways to spread the written word. From Facebook and Twitter to blogs and emails and texts and letters. From parish involvement to social group engagement. We have the power to influence countless others, through the expression of our words.

The Goal

Pope John Paul II, who was respected as "the great communicator" among many other titles, said in *Rapid Development* that "the great challenge of our time, for believers and all people of good will, is maintaining truthful and free communication," with attention, discernment and constant vigilance developing a healthy critical capacity regarding the persuasive force of the communications media." He urged believers to count on the help of the Holy Spirit in that ongoing task:

> Such help is all the more necessary when one considers how greatly the obstacles intrinsic to communication can be increased by ideologies, by the desire for profit or for power, and by rivalries and conflicts between individuals and groups, and also because of human weakness and social troubles. The modern technologies increase to a remarkable extent the speed, quantity and accessibility of communication, but they

> above all do not favor that delicate exchange which takes place between mind and mind, between heart and heart, and which should characterize any communication at the service of solidarity and love.

How eloquently John Paul stated that ultimate goal of communications media, as it was originally intended to be by the first transmission of the Word.

Contemplating the Gospel of John and remarking on John 1:11, Pope Paul VI said this in a General Audience on December 4, 1974:

> Christ came; but by a mysterious and terrible misfortune, not everyone accepted him....It is the picture of humanity before us today, after twenty centuries of Christianity. How did this happen? What shall we say? We do not claim to fathom a reality immersed in mysteries that transcend us—the mystery of good and evil. But we can recall that the economy of Christ, for its light to spread, requires a subordinate but necessary cooperation on the part of man—the cooperation of evangelization, of the apostolic and missionary Church. If there is still work to be done, it is all the more necessary for everyone to help her.

This is where the rubber meets the road. Complacency is not an option. Our voices must be heard, our witness lived and therefore, seen. You can't un-see something, and it has a great impact if it is beautiful. You can't un-ring a bell. People can't un-hear something. It will be all the more powerful in resounding in their minds and hearts, if it rings true.

People of the Word, it's time to speak.

A New Renaissance: The Church as Patroness of the Arts

By Duncan Stroik

What contributions has the Catholic Church made to society in her 2,000-year history? Many of the modern institutions that we are most proud of, colleges and hospitals in particular,[1] were founded and maintained by the Church and we are the beneficiaries today. In the world of art, architecture, and music it should be acknowledged that the Church has been a major force and patron up through the early twentieth century. In fact, it can be demonstrated that one of the major ways that the Church influenced culture historically was through the arts. We can also admit that this is no longer the case.

In the twentieth century, the arts moved away from the Church and found more appealing patrons in civic and private realms. The interest in concepts such as primitivism, the occult, abstraction, disfigurement and even iconoclasm by artists (and the elite) generally did not sit well with the Church and understandably she moved away from the world of mainstream art.

The church of Notre-Dame de Toute Grâce du Plateau d'Assy in France, completed in 1946 under the direction of Dominican Marie-Alain Couturier. Credit: www.narthex.fr

After World War II in Europe, there was an embrace of modernist art and architecture by some in the Church, as witnessed in the work commissioned by Fr. Marie-Alain Couturier, O.P. first in the parish church at Assy, France. A number of well-known modernist or unbelieving artists were commissioned to produce art, including Henri Matisse, Marc Chagall, and Fernand Léger.

The Convent Sainte-Marie de La Tourette, completed in 1960 by Le Corbusier. Credit: flickr.com/SanyamBahga

Also, at the Monastery of LaTourette, the preeminent architect of the day, Le Corbusier, was hired to invent a new type of monastery for the Dominicans. Le Corbusier's belief was not in God *per se*, but in "the religious consciousness of belonging to a greater mankind,"[2] and "the miracle of inexpressible space."[3] Fr. Couturier did not think this was a problem, saying that "excellence and artistic sincerity were... to come before faith and piety."[4]

The Cathedral of Our Lady of the Angels in Los Angeles opened in 2002. Credit: www.you-are-here.com

The situation today is complex. On the one hand we see a part of the Church that continues to take cues from secular art and architecture. This is most clear in major (and expensive) projects such as the new cathedrals in Oakland and Los Angeles, the new chapel at Ave Maria University, and the proposed renovation of a Protestant mega-church in Orange, California, into a Catholic cathedral.

On the other hand, there is a desire for traditional architecture. However, it often ends up being done in a mediocre way due to modest budgets or the limited knowledge of the artists and architects.

The Cathedral of Notre Dame in Paris was constructed from 1163-1345. Credit: Wikimedia.org

Given our present political, cultural, and religious predicaments there seem to be more important things for the Church to invest in than in the arts. So why should she? For the same reasons that the Church historically invested in the arts. The arts can be seen as that which people do with their treasure, reflecting their highest aspirations. Not only can they symbolize that which is beyond us, but art and architecture can point us away from the material towards the immaterial. It is the Church's belief that eternal truths are as true today as in the time of Christ and that modern man is in need of learning them, even if he thinks they are irrelevant. Thus, a compelling art and architecture can speak to modern man, and not necessarily in the way that he is expecting. For example, I would suggest that Notre Dame Cathedral, St. Peter's Basilica and the Sistine chapel are all recognized by modern people as beautiful, profound, and moving, whether they have faith or not.

Pope Benedict XVI dedicated the Church of Sagrada Familia in Barcelona on November 7, 2010, 128 years after construction began on the church. Credit: www.katolik-gomel.by

So where are the Notre Dame cathedrals being built today? Some would say the Sagrada Familia Basilica in Barcelona, Spain. How can we in our time offer an image of the eternal to modern man in the American context? How can we offer an image that can help to form modern man, and also help to form the art and architecture of the secular realm? If done right, great art will also speak to future generations. In order to influence the culture today I suggest we need to re-embrace the Church's role as patroness of the arts, including painting, sculpture, architecture, music, drama, and dance.

Pope Julius II ordering Bramante, Michelangelo, and Raphael to construct Vatican and St. Peter's, 1827 by Horace Vernet Credit: avito.ru

What does it mean to be a patroness of the arts? Patronage is the support and promotion of the arts; to promote high standards and support art financially. Arts patronage is crucial to the existence of many of our institutions today: museums, ballet, opera, and symphony orchestras, to name a few. So, too, it should be with the art of the Church. As patroness, the Church will focus on art in service of the Church and the liturgy, but also seek to influence the arts in all their manifestations. Nurtured by her tradition, the Church has set out a clear vision about the importance of beauty, which is appreciated in the secular realm.

Patronage should be a general goal of the Church, but in practice it is a work of individuals. We need priests, bishops, cardinals, and individual laity to re-embrace their historic role as patrons of the arts. Behind every great building there are both an architect and a patron. Behind every great public work of art there is the talented artist and the wise patron. And that doesn't mean it was easy going to work together. The Sistine Chapel ceiling is a case in point. It was an acknowledged work of genius by Michelangelo, but it is Pope Julius II who gets the credit for convincing the sculptor to pick up a paintbrush against his wishes (and then help him to create the brilliant narrative). Another example is the Medici family in Florence, who hired the top architects of their day to design their palaces, and the top painters to decorate them. They also promoted the building of one of the first new churches of the Italian Renaissance: San Lorenzo. As patrons, the Medicis also got the assistance of other families to pay for a side chapel and commission worthy artists to paint an altarpiece.

What are the things that the Church as an institution, as well as individuals, can do to promote a culture of beauty, truth, and life? I will touch on three initiatives that are desperately needed today.

I. Foster the Work of Talented Artists. As the *General Instruction of the Roman Missal* states, "in appointing artists and choosing works of art to be admitted into a church, what should be looked for is that true excellence in art which nourishes faith and devotion and accords authentically with both the meaning and the purpose for which it is intended."[5]

First, we need to search out the finest Catholic artists and give them worthy projects to work on. This is like investing in a startup company where the potential return is in the creation of beauty. We need to research and compare artists, and travel to see their buildings and their sculptures in person. The building is a sermon in stone, and the painting is a window into the divine. Since sacred art and architecture are partly a work of theology and devotion, they are best done by someone who tries to live them.

In the Old Testament, one thinks of the scriptural account of Moses hiring Bezalel to build the Tabernacle in the wilderness, which would shelter the Ark of the Covenant:

> See, the Lord has chosen Bezalel son of Uri, the son of Hur, of the tribe of Judah, and he has filled him with the Spirit of God, with wisdom, with understanding, with knowledge and with all kinds of skills— to make artistic designs for work in gold, silver and bronze, to cut and set stones, to work in wood and to engage in all kinds of artistic crafts. And he has given both him and Oholiab son of Ahisamak, of the tribe of Dan, the ability to teach others. He has filled them with skill to do all kinds of work as engravers, designers, embroiderers in blue, purple and scarlet yarn and fine linen, and weavers—all of them skilled workers and designers.[6]

The artist chosen to work for the Church should have the qualities of Bezalel: the spirit, wisdom, understanding, knowledge, and skill.

The choir of the Basilica of S. Denis was renovated in 1140 by the Abbot Suger, and it was later recognized as the first Gothic church. Credit: bluffton.edu

Abbott Suger is credited with being the patron of the first fully Gothic building, the abbey church of Saint Denis where the Kings of France were buried. In Suger's *De Administratione,* he writes, "because of the age of the old walls and their impending ruin in some places, we summoned the best painters I could find from different regions, and reverently caused these to be repaired and becomingly painted with gold and precious colors."[7] This is the nature of the Patron: to seek out and choose the best artists and architects.

The patron will educate himself about the artist's work and about art in general. The way to become a connoisseur of sacred art and architecture is through reading, travel, and spending time contemplating art. This will help you to converse with the artist and architect and make you a better client. The more you know about art, the more you will appreciate true talent and the hard work it takes to produce it, and the more you will give good feedback during the creation of art. That is because making art is a process and the true patron has active participation (though not control of) the process.

Dr. Tom Dillon, then-President of Thomas Aquinas College in California, met with Pope John Paul II in the Vatican to show him the design of the college's planned new chapel. The Pope also blessed the cornerstone of the chapel. Credit: Duncan G. Stroik Architect, LLC

A patron is like the patron saint who helps us in our professions and in our lives. The patron spends time with the artist looking at his art, discussing it and its relation to theology. He can help deepen the artist's theological knowledge and at the same time allow the artist to deepen his knowledge of art. This means spending time with the architect, visiting historic buildings, visiting carving workshops, and choosing materials. Of course, all of this entails a substantial commitment of time and resources.

When the artist is young, encourage him to stick close to the tradition and seek for excellence. When the artist is mature and knows the tradition, challenge him to innovate upon it. Push the artist to go beyond what he knows and has done before so as to produce his best work yet. At the same time, give him respect and trust. As one of my clients once said, "I always want to know what you think. Please tell me when you think we are going in the wrong direction." In moments of indecision or disagreement, trust the artist. By all means, show the artist your favorite paintings of the Madonna or façades of churches, but don't require him to copy it. Allow the artist to create a relative of the great works of art, not a clone.

II. Create a Market for Great Religious Art. In order for the Church to form the culture, she needs to be seen as producing the best art and architecture today, works that cannot be ignored. But how can we get the best artwork? We need the best artists and architects to see the Church as a great client and to want to work for her. This can be accomplished only by making sacred art attractive to top artists and architects.

Bishop Paul Swain of the Diocese of Sioux Falls, South Dakota, meets with sculptor Cody Swanson to review work for the renovation of the Cathedral of St. Joseph in Sioux Falls. Credit: Duncan G. Stroik Architect, LLC

Half of the answer is financial—to have generous budgets for our buildings and artwork and to pay artists better than they are paid in the secular realm. Unfortunately, if we do the opposite, we will get what we pay for. This was explained to me many years ago by a famous structural engineer, who said that churches are such terrible clients that when church committees came knocking on his door he would give them money and recommend they hire his competitors.

Raymond Cardinal Burke, patron of the Shrine of Our Lady of Guadalupe in La Crosse, Wisconsin, visits the church during construction. Credit: Duncan G. Stroik Architect, LLC

The reality is that we often expect artists and architects to work for the Church for the love of it. We think of them as a commodity, and choose them based on the lowest price. This is not a recipe for creating a masterpiece that the world will notice. Top artists and architects working in the secular realm are paid as well as those in other specialized, highly skilled professions. In the past, the greatest artists, architects and musicians worked for the Church in part or in full. Today, the Church shows how much it values the arts by not hiring the best and not being willing to pay top dollar. Great art takes great talent, and it also takes time. And the only way an artist can afford to do great work is to spend the time necessary and to be remunerated for it.

Another way to entice artists and architects is to bring a sense of competition to working for the Church, in which the artist is straining to build the most majestic exterior, the tallest interior, the most spiritual iconography and the most beautiful building possible. Works of art should be out of the ordinary, of the highest artistic standards and with the largest budgets. They are like the expensive ointment the woman in the Gospels anoints Christ's feet with, not just some cheap oil bought from the drugstore.

Medieval altarpieces on display at the Victoria and Albert Museum in London. Credit: www.bugbog.com

Our art museums recognize the importance of historic sacred art. Are we patronizing anything good enough today that people would go out of their way to visit or that would be worthy of an art museum?

The architecture of our churches is very public and has the potential to lift up the architecture of the neighborhood, of the city, and of the region. Why aren't the top classical architects fighting to work for the Church? The answer is that the Church is not seen as a patron. She has been replaced by museums, universities, corporations, and private individuals. The Church seems to require low architects' fees and budgets that prevent her from building as she did in past ages.

What are some practical ways to create a market for sacred art? Perhaps competitions for sacred art and architecture could help promote excellence and inspire artists to participate. Quality artwork requires generous fees and buildings with budgets that allow the architect to use the finest in classic materials: marble, stone, bronze, onyx, cast iron, gold leaf, and slate.

The parish church of the Holy Family in Chicago is located next to St. Ignatius College Prep, whose main building dates from before the Chicago fire of 1871. Credit: flickr.com/Jesuits

And all of our Catholic buildings should speak the language of beauty, permanence, and transcendence. If we value education, catechesis, and our pastors, then we will build schools, halls, and rectories with custom art and architecture that reflects those values. Instead we follow the secular culture in our ancillary buildings by demanding quantity (rather than quality) at minimal cost. It was not too long ago that the art and architecture of the Catholic parish and the Catholic university campus sought to be timeless.

III. Establish a Sacred Art Academy at a University. A third way we can promote a culture of beauty is to establish a college-level sacred art academy. Its purpose would be to create a supply of Catholic artists who can serve both the Church and the secular realm.

Of the two hundred Catholic colleges and universities in America only three teach architecture. Of those two hundred colleges and universities there are numerous departments of art, but I am not aware of any that are considered top in their field. This is strange for the sponsoring institution that has been at the forefront of art and architecture in her 2000-year history. There are reasons, of course, why poor immigrants in America did not focus on training students in art and architecture. Perhaps there was even the sense in the late nineteenth and early twentieth centuries that secular schools were doing a pretty good job of it—and they were. There is also the reality that the Irish who largely ran the Church in America did not come from a culture that had a strength in art, architecture, and music. This was due in part to the oppression of Irish Catholics by their English overlords.[8]

I propose an art school with a theological vision to train artists in the Western tradition while studying Catholic theories about art. This classical vision would ground them in the figure, the artistic patrimony of the Church, and the integration of art with architecture. The faculty would be made up of experienced artists who are working for the Church and for the public, and who have expertise in the arts central to sacred buildings: oil painting, fresco, sculpture in metal and stone, mosaic, and stained glass. Students would draw from casts and from life as has been the tradition since the Renaissance. Anatomy and perspective would be taught. Art students would also gain a basic competency in drawing traditional architecture so that they could collaborate with architects.

American artist Anthony Visco works on a painting for the Shrine of Our Lady of Guadalupe in La Crosse, Wisconsin. Credit: anthonyvisco.org

A museum of great works of art should be nearby so the students could draw upon it. A travel semester to France or Italy should be required. One exciting development is the Sacred Art Academy in Florence, founded and run by American artist Anthony Visco. Recently, the Academy offered a summer course on painting the Annunciation and the Last Supper. In Florence you can study ten of the best Annunciation paintings of all time while creating your own—which is an example of the type of program a Catholic art school could offer.

Students at the Grand Central Atelier in New York work on a four-hour portrait sketch session. Credit: Grand Central Atelier, NYC, 2014

The goal of the Sacred Art Academy is threefold: 1) Train students who can produce Catholic art at the highest level; 2) Give artists a theological vision for ennobling our artistic culture; and 3) Give artists the ability to create classical art for the secular realm. This classical vision is still desired by many Americans, as evidenced by the recent Eisenhower Memorial debates in Washington, DC.[9]

One of the reasons I believe that this can be accomplished, and that a school like this can have a national impact on the Church and the secular realm is that it has happened before. We see examples throughout history, from the academy at Villa Medici where Michelangelo trained, to the French École de Beaux-Arts where Ingres taught, to the Pennsylvania Art Academy and other schools in America, which trained generations of great artists. These schools, with talented professors and students, carried on great work and serious debate that affected the culture. Judging by the number of small classical ateliers across the country today, I believe there is a groundswell of interest amongst artists and art students for such a classical academy for our time.

The second reason I believe founding an academy of sacred art is possible is that it has recently been done in the world of architecture. In 1989, Thomas Gordon Smith began to radically transform the University of Notre Dame School of Architecture into a classical program. He had pushback at first from the older faculty and students, but after bringing in new faculty and re-focusing the school (including revamping the year spent in Rome), it has been a big success for the secular culture and for the Church. When I graduated from architecture school in 1987, there were no more than ten classical architecture firms I knew of in the United States. Now, thirty years later there are over one hundred. This is not a result simply of demand, but has been caused in part by forty classically trained architecture graduates entering the profession each year. Certainly, the production of art is different than architecture, but I believe the Notre Dame School of Architecture is a model that could be emulated at a Catholic art school.

In conclusion: I suggest that the Church become patroness of the arts once again. To do this she should start with what she knows best—sacred art and architecture. Three ways to begin are to foster the work of individual artists, to create a market for high quality sacred art, and to create a supply of classically trained Catholic artists.

Fr. Patrick Doolan works on a fresco of the Pantocrator in St. Seraphim of Sarov Orthodox Church, Santa Rosa, California. The dome frescos were completed in July 2014. Credit: orthodoxartsjournal.org

A new fresco by Raúl Berzosa, *Crowning of the Virgin Mary*, covers the ceiling of the Santa Maria Reina Oratory in Málaga, Spain. Credit: Raúl Berzosa

A side shrine dedicated to St. Maria Goretti at the Shrine of Our Lady of Guadalupe in La Crosse, Wisconsin. Painting by Noah Buchanan, completed in 2008. Credit: tumblr_n2i6fj7RM91s9od7wo6_500

A side shrine dedicated to St. Gianna Beretta Molla at the Shrine of Our Lady of Guadalupe in La Crosse, Wisconsin. Painting by Neilson Carlin, completed in 2008. Credit: Duncan G. Stroik Architect. LLC

A new reredos and painting of the *Assumption of the Blessed Virgin* by Leonard Porter was the final phase in a renovation of St. Mary Church in Norwalk, Connecticut, completed in 2013. Credit: John Canning

Notes

[1] Also, we would include orphanages, unwed mothers homes, houses for young women, etc.

[2] Martin Purdy, "Le Corbusier and the Theological Program," *The Open Hand, Essays on Le Corbusier* (Cambridge: MIT Press, 1986), 289, cited by Denis McNamara, "'Almost Religious': Couturier, Le Corbusier and the Monastery of La Tourette," *Sacred Architecture*, vol. 2, 22-26, 23.

[3] Purdy, 299, cited by McNamara, 26.

[4] Purdy, 293, cited by McNamara, 23.

[5] *General Instruction of the Roman Missal* 289. The *GIRM* here cites *Sacrosanctum concilium* 123: "The Church has not adopted any particular style of art as her very own; she has admitted styles from every period according to the natural talents and circumstances of peoples, and the needs of the various rites. Thus, in the course of the centuries, she has brought into being a treasury of art which must be very carefully preserved. The art of our own days, coming from every race and region, shall also be given free scope in the Church, provided that it adorns the sacred buildings and holy rites with due reverence and honor; thereby it is enabled to contribute its own voice to that wonderful chorus of praise in honor of the Catholic faith sung by great men in times gone by."

[6] Exodus 35:30-35

[7] Abbott Suger, *De Administratione*, XXIV: Of the Church's Decoration.

[8] See Thomas Day, *Why Catholics Can't Sing: The Culture of Catholicism and the Triumph of Bad Taste*. New York: Crossroad, 2000 reprint edition (1990 original).

[9] For one discussion of the debates, see Clem Labine, "End of the the Line for Gehry's Eisenhower Memorial," The CIVITAS Chronicles, Traditional Building Online, traditional-building.com/clem_labine/?p=911.

Restoring American Law

By Lawrence M. Stratton

On Monday September 17, 1787 after the Constitutional Convention approved the original U.S. Constitution on Benjamin Franklin's motion, James Madison recorded that "[t]he members then proceeded to sign the instrument."[1] As the last members affixed their signatures to the document, Benjamin Franklin said that he had wondered during the "vicissitudes of my hopes and fears" as the convention proceeded whether the half-sun on the back of the President's Chair was a "rising or setting" sun.[2] "But now, at length," Franklin declared, "I have the happiness to know that it is a rising and not a setting sun."[3] Our task is to keep the U.S. Constitution's light shining.

Oliver Wendell Holmes, Jr. wrote in his famous 1897 *Harvard Law Review* essay "The Path of the Law" that "[t]he law is the witness and external deposit of our moral life."[4] "Its history is the history of the moral development of the race," Holmes observed.[5] A few pages later Holmes said, "The prophecies of what the courts will do in fact, and nothing more pretentious, are what I mean by the law."[6] Those dissatisfied with law's path trace the trend lines of future judicial decision-making and the entire government edifice and do not like what they see on the horizon.

Each judge and each justice is a product of a confluence of political factors of a specific historical moment that profoundly impacts society's next generation. Constitutional law would presumably be different today had Robert Bork ascended to the U.S. Supreme Court rather than Anthony Kennedy in 1987.[7] *Planned Parenthood of Southeastern Pennsylvania v. Casey*,[8] which largely affirmed *Roe v. Wade*[9] in 1992, would presumably have had a different holding. Of course, President George H.W. Bush's two Justices—David Souter and Clarence Thomas—split their votes in that case. Justices appointed by

Presidents Bill Clinton and Barack Obama necessarily differ from those who might have been appointed by Robert Dole or John McCain.

Even if the Supreme Court, as Finley Peter Dunne's character Mr. Dooley put it, "follows th' iliction returns,"[10] all is not lost. The dynamic structure of the U.S. Constitution itself provides the basis for its renewal. Franklin said that despite the "prejudices," "passions," "errors of opinion," "local interests," and "selfish views," of his fellow framers, "It therefore astonishes me, sir, to find this system approaching so near to perfection as it does...."[11] It would have been fascinating to have had an off-the-record conversation with the author and publisher of *Poor Richard's Almanac* to get his assessment of the strengths and weaknesses of each constitutional clause, all premised upon the sovereignty of "We the People."

What did Franklin think of the views of another Pennsylvanian named William Penn who believed that good government required a combination of good laws and good men? As Penn wrote in his *Preface to the First Frame of Government of Pennsylvania* in 1682:

> Governments, like clocks, go from the motion men give them, and as governments are made and moved by men, so by them they are ruined too. Wherefore governments rather depend upon men than men upon governments. Let men be good and the government cannot be bad: if it be ill, they will cure it. But if men be bad, let the government be never so good, they will endeavor to warp and spoil it to their turn.[12]

The challenge facing Christians and all Americans in our own historical moment is to "cure" and restore the original principles expressed in the U.S. Constitution.

Twentieth century theologian Reinhold Niebuhr wrote this in his late 1930s treatise, *The Nature and Destiny of Man*: "It is the highest achievement of democratic societies that they embody the principle of resistance to government within the principle of government itself."[13] Niebuhr noted that citizens are armed with "'constitutional' power to resist the unjust exactions of government" without creating anarchy.[14] The political and legal errors of our contemporary Republic can be resisted and reformed *within* the constitutional system. It is hard work, but it is a worthy task.

Echoing the Constitution's framers, Niebuhr wrote that "[i]t may be taken as axiomatic that great disproportions of power lead to injustice, whatever the efforts to mitigate it."[15] Niebuhr says that the U.S. Constitution's underlying political philosophy "is characterized by a shrewd awareness of the potential conflicts of power and passion in every community."[16] Imbued with this underlying philosophy, he observes, "The Constitution protects the citizen against abuses of government, not so much by keeping government weak as by introducing the principle of balance of power into government."[17]

The U.S. Constitution's structural protections against power concentration sought to "tame the prince" as Harvey C. Mansfield, Jr. put it,[18] by dividing the powers of government so that, as James Madison wrote in Federalist Paper #51, "Ambition must be made to counteract ambition" to prevent any faction from dominating the whole.[19] This can be seen in the separation of powers between the executive, legislative, and judicial branches in the Federal Government, which is, in turn, replicated in the extended Republic that balances state and federal powers.[20] The constitutional rubric thus provides structural protections against the concentration of power as every power center is checked and balanced.

Echoing Niebuhr, Professor Marci A. Hamilton of the Benjamin N. Cardozo School of Law has traced the U.S. Constitution's system of checks and balances to Calvinist thought, which held that "man's will is corrupt by nature but also capable of doing good," a view that permeated the Founding era and influenced Madison and other members of the Constitutional Convention who were students of Declaration of Independence signer and Presbyterian minister, the Rev. John Witherspoon, President of the College of New Jersey, now Princeton University.[21] In her essay, "The Calvinist Paradox of Distrust and Hope at the Constitutional Convention," published in the 2001 Yale University Press anthology *Christian Perspectives on Legal Thought*, edited by Michael W. McConnell, Hamilton describes how the Constitutional Convention was "a contest in distrust" to prevent the proposed government from tyrannically overstepping its bounds: "Following the teachings of Rev. John Witherspoon, they believed that properly structured governing institutions could deter overreaching if not wholly prevent it."[22]

Regardless of the philosophical *and theological* origins of the U.S. Constitution's system of checks and balances, which also has Enlightenment roots,[23] the immensity of the Federal government and its vast administrative structure today make it largely unchecked and unbalanced. University of Pennsylvania constitutional scholar Richard Beeman wrote in the *Penguin Guide to the United States Constitution* that Article I section 8's list of Federal government powers "constitute's the heart and soul of the U.S. Constitution" because "[i]t specifically enumerates the powers that the federal government is permitted to exercise."[24] But the elasticity of the list of enumerated powers, the catch-all "necessary and proper" clause, and judicial stretching as in Chief Justice John Roberts's *NFIB v. Sebelius* opinion upholding Obamacare's health insurance mandate by recasting a penalty as a tax,[25] limit the section's use as a limitation of federal authority.

James Madison's theory that the division of powers within the government would protect liberty as the branches of government competed with one another as ambition would counter ambition has not worked as planned. University of Chicago Law Professor Eric A. Posner and Harvard Law Professor Adrian Vermeule state in their 2013 Oxford University Press book, *The Executive Unbound: After the Madisonian Republic* that "[t]he Madisonian framework is broken and cannot be translated or otherwise adapted to the administrative state…."[26]

In defiance of the Anglo-Saxon legal maxim *Delegata potestas non potest delegari*—"A delegated power cannot itself be delegated"—the vast number of rules of conduct under which citizens are forced to live do not derive from accountable legislators, but from administrative agencies which interpret broadly worded statutes.[27] New York Law School professor David Schoenbrod shows in his 1993 book, *Power Without Responsibility: How Congress Abuses the People Through Delegation*, that the American people are no longer governed by statutory law enacted by legislators who are accountable to them.[28] In his new book, *Our Lost Constitution: The Willful Subversion of America's Founding Document*, Utah Senator Mike Lee notes that the ratio of pages of federal laws passed by Congress in 2013 compared to the regulations proposed and adopted by federal administrative agencies in 2013 was eight hundred to eighty thousand, thus suggesting that unelected bureaucrats write ninety-nine percent of the federal rules by which Americans must live.[29]

Why did members of the Congressional branch surrender legislative power? The pattern seems to be that as the crisis of the day creates a political movement for Congress to do something, often at the prodding of a President, Congress passes a statute—however vague—just to say that it did. This sentiment was evident in House Speaker Nancy Pelosi's statement that Congress "[has] to pass the [healthcare] bill so you can find out what's in it, away from the fog of controversy."[30] If a bill was too specific, Congress might have to bear the political cost if the statute were to become unpopular. At the other end of Pennsylvania Avenue at the White House, the President would prefer a vague or open-ended statute so that he or she could more readily rewrite it in the administrative rule-making process, covered by the political fallback of blaming Congress for the statute's ambiguity. If the executive action is ever challenged in the judiciary, the courts are likely to let the other branches fight it out with judicial pronouncements such as "the administrative interpretation of the act by the enforcing agency is entitled to great deference" and other similar refrains which culminated in the famous 1980s *Chevron* doctrine in which the U.S. Supreme Court gave wide statutory interpretive latitude to executive agencies.[31]

Posner and Vermeule go so far as to say that, "researchers should no longer view American political life through the Madisonian prism, while normative theorists should cease bemoaning the decline of Madisonianism and instead make peace with the new political order."[32] They boldly declare:

> The center of gravity has shifted to the executive, which both makes policy and administers it, subject to weak constraints imposed by Congress, the judiciary, and the states. It is pointless to bewail these developments, and futile to argue that Madisonian structures should be reinvigorated. Instead, attention should shift to the political constraints on the president and the institutions through which those political constraints operate—chief among them elections, parties, bureaucracy, and the media.[33]

Posner and Vermeule even posit that the "centuries-old British parliamentary system" which depends on public opinion "should provide reason for optimism."[34] They provocatively conclude, "The British record on executive abuses, although hardly perfect, is no worse than the American record and arguably better, despite the lack of Madisonian separation of legislative and executive powers."[35]

This posited philosophical shift from across the Atlantic to the supremacy of the English Parliament with its unity between executive and legislative branches seems radical. Structurally the U.S. Capitol, White House, and Supreme Court will remain three distinct entities and locations in Washington, D.C., however intermeshed, with administrative agencies placed throughout the Capital Beltway. Still, Posner and Vermeule's descriptive assessment helps us answer H. Richard Niebuhr's first question in Christian ethical analysis, "What is going on?"[36] They recognize that their call for a more organic approach to "power sharing and constraint" apart from the "clockwork mechanism bequeathed to us by the Enlightenment thinking of the founders" may require more public attention than can be expected, "but the old system of checks and balances always depended on public opinion as well," they note.[37]

And that's the critical point. The values and principles in the U.S. Constitution are not good because they are in the U.S. Constitution. They are good in and of themselves because they reside within the hearts and souls of the American people. Our public discourse might be stronger and less shrill if we had more thorough and less heated public discussions about the policy contours of privacy, contract, speech, property, criminal procedure, religious establishment and free exercise, and civil rights without having to resort to the courts where judges at times arbitrarily apply complex webs of constitutional scrutiny levels and balancing tests. The classic law school constitutional conundrum for those who accept Justice Oliver Wendell Holmes, Jr.'s statement rejecting the Supreme Court's embrace of "Liberty of Contract" in the *Lochner* case striking down New York's weekly hours limitations on bakers—"The 14th Amendment does not enact Mr. Herbert Spencer's Social Statics"[38]—is whether Justice William O. Douglas was "*Lochnerizing*" when he found an unenumerated constitutional right to privacy, saying "specific guarantees in the Bill of Rights have penumbras, formed by emanations from those guarantees that help give them life and substance" in *Griswold v. Connecticut.*[39] Some students embrace *Lochner* and reject *Griswold*, while others accept both. Lost in the fray is a solid and thoroughgoing discussion of the proper scope of government regulation of economic and social endeavor.

If we continue our discussions and engage our fellow citizens about the proper vision of freedom, liberty, equality before the law, and other great constitutional principles, informed by the Declaration of Independence and the tyranny it protested, we can realistically share Benjamin Franklin's optimism that the American constitutional system is a rising sun.

Notes

[1] Edward J. Larson and Michael P. Winship, *The Constitutional Convention: A Narrative History from the Notes of James Madison* (New York: Modern Library, 2005), 156.

[2] Ibid.

[3] Ibid.

[4] Oliver Wendell Holmes, Jr., "The Path of the Law" *Harvard Law Review*, vol. X no. 8 (March 25, 1897): 61, 459.

[5] Ibid.

[6] Ibid., 461.

[7] *See generally*, Jan Crawford Greenberg, *Supreme Conflict: The Inside Story of the Struggle for Control of the United States Supreme Court* (New York: Penguin Press, 2007), 46-63.

[8] *Planned Parenthood of Southeastern Pennsylvania v. Casey*, 505 U.S. 833 (1992).

[9] *Roe v. Wade*, 410 U.S. 113 (1973).

[10] *Mr. Dooley's Opinions* (New York: R.H. Russell, 1901), 26; *See*, Edward J. Bander, *Mr. Dooley & Mr. Dunne: The Literary Life of a Chicago Catholic* (Charlottesville, VA: Michie Law Publishers, 1981).

[11] Larson and Winship, *Constitutional Convention*, 154.

[12] William Penn, "Preface to the First Frame of Government of Pennsylvania" in Isaac Kramnick and Theodore J. Lowi, eds., *American Political Thought: A Norton Anthology* (New York: W.W. Norton & Company, 2009), 82.

[13] Reinhold Niebuhr, *The Nature and Destiny of Man, Volume II: Human Destiny* (1943; repr., Louisville, KY: Westminster John Knox Press, 1996), 268.

[14] Ibid.

[15] Niebuhr, *Nature and Destiny*, 262.

[16] Reinhold Niebuhr, *The Irony of American History* (New York: Scribner's, 1952), 98.

[17] Ibid., 97.

[18] Harvey C. Mansfield, Jr. *Taming the Prince: The Ambivalence of Modern Executive Power* (Baltimore and London: Johns Hopkins University Press, 1993).

[19] James Madison "Federalist Paper #51" in George W. Carey and James McClellan eds., *The Federalist* (Indianapolis: Liberty Fund, 2001), 268.

[20] George W. Carey, *In Defense of the Constitution* Rev. ed. (Indianapolis, IN: Liberty Fund, 1995), 34-52.

[21] Marci A. Hamilton, "The Calvinist Paradox of Distrust and Hope at the Constitutional Convention" in Michael W. McConnell, ed., *Perspectives on Legal Thought* (New Haven, CT: Yale Univ. Press, 2001), 294.

[22] Ibid., 298.

[23] John M. Murrin, "Religion and Politics in America from the First Settlements to the Civil War" in Mark A. Noll, ed., *Religion and American Politics: From the Colonial Period to the 1980s* (New York: Oxford Univ. Press, 1990), 31.

[24] Richard Beeman, *The Penguin Guide to the United States Constitution* (New York: Penguin Books, 32.

[25] *National Federation of Independent Business v. Sebelius*, 567 U.S. ___ (2012), 132 S.Ct. 2566.

[26] Eric A. Posner and Adrian Vermeule, *The Executive Unbound: After the Madisonian Republic* (New York: Oxford University Press, 2010), 15.

[27] Paul Craig Roberts and Lawrence M. Stratton, *The Tyranny of Good Intentions: How Prosecutors and Law Enforcement are Trampling the Constitution in the Name of Justice* (New York: Three Rivers Press, 2008), 157.

[28] David Schoenbrod, *Power Without Responsibility: How Congress Abuses the People Through Delegation* (Yale University Press, 1993).

[29] Mike Lee, *Our Lost Constitution: The Willful Subversion of America's Founding Document* (New York: Penguin Sentinel, 2015), 7.

[30] Peter Roff, "Pelosi: Pass Health Reform So You Can Find Out What's In It: The Speaker Has a Surprise for Voters," *US News and World Report*, 9 March 2010.

[31] *Chevron U.S.A., Inc. v. Natural Resources Defense Council, Inc.*, 467 U.S. 837 (1984).

[32] Posner and Vermeule, *Executive Unbound*, 209.

[33] Ibid.

[34] Ibid., 210.

[35] Ibid.

[36] H. Richard Niebuhr, *The Responsible Self: An Essay in Christian Moral Philosophy* (New York: Harper & Row, 1978), 60.

[37] Posner and Vermeule, *Executive Unbound*, 209-210.

[38] *Lochner v. New York*, 198 U.S. 45, 75 (1905)(Holmes, J., dissenting).

[39] *Griswold v. Connecticut*, 381 U.S. 479, 484 (1965).

Restoring Sound Culture and American Principles: The Different Dimensions of a Social and Political Response

By Stephen M. Krason

The first question one might ask is whether it is correct to speak about restoring sound culture and American principles in the same breath. After all, didn't Aristotle emphasize that there were deficiencies in almost all political orders, that while the best political order was conceivable none in existence measured up to the standards of goodness per se? Further, aren't we discussing how to reverse the cultural decay that especially afflicts not just the United States but also other Western countries? True enough, but even taking into account the blemishes in the American Founding itself, our parchment Republic and the culture that spawned it—as I have argued elsewhere—were not just sound, but exemplary. The American Republic was truly "a new order for the ages." [1] The great American Catholic political thinker Orestes Augustus Brownson, according to Fr. Americo Lapati (one of the leading scholars of Brownson), believed that "America's special political mission to the world" was how it successfully balanced in its constitutional republic "equal individual rights and the powers of government."[2] That is, it resolved better than previous political orders the fundamental problem of insuring that government would have enough power to carry out its rightful functions, while still protecting the rights of its citizens. The meaning of all this is that when we talk about restoring sound culture, it can rightfully be said that in many respects it involves restoring the cultural conditions of our Founding Era and—in terms of politics, law, and constitutionalism—the principles set down by our Founding Fathers.

A Crisis of Reason

Sound culture and the American political tradition are erected on the foundation of reason. We cannot underestimate the extent to which the crisis of contemporary culture is a crisis of reason, resulting from an assault on reason and the elevation of the will driven by the passions to a position of preeminence in the lives of both individuals and political societies. One among a multitude of examples is seen in the notion of "post-humanism," which is the domination of individual wills over human nature, with the result that the notion of human rights as enshrined in the great international human rights documents of the first half of the twentieth century and foreshadowed by the U.S. Constitution and Bill of Rights has given way to a rank individualist notion of rights. The latter often concerns nothing more than desires, no matter how base or how unreflectively embraced. Such a new conception of rights is now driving the decision-making of major international human rights tribunals, such as the European Court of Human Rights.[3] It has also shaped the jurisprudence of the U.S. Supreme Court for the last four decades or more. The Court basically expressed the thinking behind this in the famous "mystery passage" in its opinion in *Planned Parenthood of Southeastern Pennsylvania v. Casey* (1992): "At the heart of liberty is the right to define one's own concept of existence, of meaning, of the universe, and of the mystery of human life."[4] The defining principle for courts and human rights tribunals now seems to be personal autonomy, whether or not it conforms to reason, a correct understanding of human nature, and the natural law tradition that has grown up with them.[5] Robert P. George has identified the almost single-minded focus on autonomy as essentially the centerpiece of many of the most influential contemporary political and legal thinkers.[6]

The struggle to restore sound culture, then, is a struggle to restore reason. It is, in effect, a battle against a condition and the profound consequences of a condition that has been five hundred years in the making, which has upset the proper ordering of the soul that Socrates and Plato spoke of: where its reasoned part is supposed to control, by bringing the will over to its side, the passions. It now rushes headlong into a more and more evident situation of nihilism. While there may be different approaches, strategies, and ways of "facing off" against the secular culture and securing cultural renewal, their objective at bottom must be to get people to think correctly—or, perhaps, to learn for the first time simply *how to think*. The appeal always must be to what is reasonable (i.e., what accords with right reason). I once heard the expression that "the natural law works in men." So the defenders of sound culture must proceed with the belief that at some level—it will not be a deep intellectual level for most—people will be moved by appeals to reason, to "the better angels of their nature." That means having the facts, making the good arguments (and knowing how to counter those of the adversary), always acting with an educative intent and spirit, mastering rhetorical practice (but not being untruthful or manipulative), making the case repeatedly and being persistently assertive so that the adversary is not allowed to define the terms of the debate, and always demonstrating courage in both small and large encounters and in big and little ways. The forces of the secular culture are descending to an ever more irrational and destructive level and exhibit an ever more intolerant and oppressive posture, but in doing so they plant the seeds of their collapse. We must believe that a vigorous, persistent, reasonable appeal—always with the requisite prudence, astuteness, and good judgment (we must always be "as gentle as doves, but as wily as serpents"), along with a proper coordination of our efforts when needed and always an abundance of prayer and an active sacramental life—will eventually bear good fruit. History shows that cultural renewal is possible, as figures like the great twentieth-century conservative thinker Russell Kirk—conservatism at its best—were fond of reminding us.

Individuals, Families, and Citizen Action[7]

With an understanding that appealing to reason, to educating in the broad sense of the word, must be our objective, the struggle to restore sound culture must take place at different levels in different arenas (with efforts both small and large). I like the expression "the fish rots from the read," which I attribute to Robert R. Reilly from an interview with him that I read about from his early days with the Intercollegiate Studies Institute. Our current cultural turmoil had its roots mostly in troublesome attitudes and beliefs. So, there is a need to alter and correct these, and that of course is not a quick or easy task. Primarily in my book, *The Transformation of the American Democratic Republic* (Chapter 10), but also in my "Neither Left nor Right, but Catholic" column that appears in *Crisis* and *The Wanderer*, I have discussed this. In the book (most of what follows in this section first appeared there), I specifically talked about what I thought were modest, doable initiatives to undertake that could, as I put it, "begin to forge a foundation for restoration" of our compromised American Founding principles and, more precisely, the culture that helped to spawn them.[8] A number of things can be done at the personal, family, and individual citizen level.

First, people should watch television less, and instead read good, old books—from the era before political correctness and erroneous revisionism—such as short historical studies of the forming of the Constitution, biographies of the Founding Fathers, and even fictional works such as *Johnny Tremain* (these instruct in a basic, often indirect way about America's heritage and basic principles). They should also watch old movies, say, from the 1930s to the 1950s because they convey the sense of personal restraint and propriety that must be re-instilled to begin the rebuilding of a culture like that of the Founding (cultures, of course, are constructed from the personal level upward). Even more basically, people need to reorient themselves—make sure of their own moral compass—and also make sure their children have the proper sense of correct attitudes and conduct for life. Turning to good books can help here again. When Allan Bloom wrote *The Closing of the American Mind*, he said that the Great Books were always available to help college students get themselves back on track in terms of intellectual and moral formation.[9] We cannot expect the general population to sink their teeth into the heavy works that, frankly, only certain college students can handle well, but there are others that are more appropriate. A good suggestion is a book like William J. Bennett's noted edited volume, *The Book of Virtues: A Treasury of Great Moral Stories.*[10] When we speak about children, concerned parents these days simply have to be prepared to do a lot of educating of their children on their own. Homeschooling is a good solution for parents who can undertake it—there is little doubt, by the way, about how successful homeschooling is for academic formation[11]—but otherwise they must closely monitor what their children are being taught in schools and supplement and provide what they are not receiving. Parents should be prepared to provide individually or get together with similarly concerned parents to provide such additional instruction through group study in such areas as: literature; American history, heritage, and government; and the history of Western civilization. Such informal, cooperative arrangements would be good for parents themselves, say, to further their own cultural and citizenship education (e.g., study groups on literary classics or on the Constitution).

To restore sound culture, people have to become reoriented to virtue. They must go against the overwhelming drift of the age toward the easy, undemanding life and commit themselves to the admittedly arduous effort of leading virtuous lives. An important part of this, when we think back to the Founding Era with its admonition against luxury and its appropriate restraints on economic freedom in the name of the common good, is to seek less in the way of material goods and be more restrained in their spending and willingness to incur debt. Americans could do well to take to heart the urging of Pope St. John Paul II to live more restrained "lifestyles"—that is, to have and use material goods in a reasonable and not excessive or superfluous manner.[12] Related to this is the need for people to restrain themselves about what they seek from government. In an era of entitlements, they should take as little as they have to from it. Not only will this help in developing more self-restraint, but also enhance a spirit of independence and self-sufficiency (both of which were a part of the early American culture that spawned our democratic republican form of government).[13]

American citizens must resolve to take the time and make the effort—actually, not a great amount of either is required—to seek more information about public issues from more sources, so they can make a more correct assessment of them as citizens. Too often, public decisions are driven by public sentiment and opinion fashioned by vague impressions of things or incomplete information with unfortunate consequences. To simply seek more information—sound bites simply are not enough—is itself an example of the enhanced citizenship education that is needed today, and it happens simply by self-initiative. Along with this, Americans concerned about restoration must take the next step—preferably with some consistency—of letting public officials know their views. Today, this can be as simple as sending an email. When enough citizens communicate with them on something, it likely will affect their actions on most things. Since the stakes are so high today, they must resolve to do this consistently and ask their like-minded friends to do the same. It almost goes without saying that citizens must then take the next—also fairly simple—step after that: voting. They should go even further: they should talk about issues of public concern more, with fellow citizens when the opportunity arises (it's not a time to follow the practice of "not discussing religion and politics") and by writing "letters to the editor" in their local newspapers. They should also make a point of showing up at candidate forums during election campaigns and at town halls that their Congressmen and state legislators have and forthrightly but politely express their views on moral and other issues affecting the culture.

Since most people gain their moral formation through religion[14]—the Founders believed that religion was crucial to sustaining a democratic republic like the U.S.[15]—and a turning from religion is a crucial factor in cultural decline,[16] there is unlikely to be a serious cultural rejuvenation without the resurgence of genuine religion. Since religious belief is fundamentally personal, this must start with each individual. Piety is, of course, a virtue—the classics recognized this and for Christianity, the highest virtues are the theological ones—one of which is faith. A virtue is a habit, and habits must be developed. So, Americans need to develop the habit of religious practice—for their political order and mostly for themselves. Like all habits, it requires discipline—not an overwhelming amount, but at least a modicum. They need to make at least a little time daily—perhaps just a few minutes—for prayer; they will not be able to avoid an excessive fixation on material things or a veritable servitude to the here-and-now without making room for the transcendent. The discipline also involves their attending church. This is crucial for their moral formation, their being clear about what that moral formation requires, and their placing religion in its proper context of communal worship of God by men who share a common "createdness" and thus an essential equality (this kind of understanding of equality is at the core of a sound culture and of the Founding conception). Moreover, they need to find a traditional church or congregation to worship in—that is, one that has not sought to accommodate itself to the cultural and intellectual trends of our era.

There is another aspect of discipline that the ordinary citizen needs to exert. The corrupted, nihilistic popular culture of contemporary America has eviscerated sound sexual morality and such norms as gentlemanliness, civility, and good manners—all of which were part of Founding Era American culture and characterize any sound culture.[17] Much of this corruption, of course, comes from the artistic community. Its sustenance depends in large part on people watching its television shows, going to its movies, reading its books, periodicals, and tabloids, and attending its plays. Curiosity, even for gossipy and lurid information, a desire to experience what others are talking about, sensual temptation, and simple boredom motivates people to indulge in this popular culture. Persons who see the problem with the popular culture should discipline themselves not to indulge in it, and encourage others to follow the same course. In fact, they could in their own small ways make alternatives for themselves and their families, as we see with such activities as Civil War era balls and cotillion dances that groups of parents in local communities organize for teenagers and pre-teens that provide a setting to develop some of the very inter-personal norms that the popular culture spurns.

To in a small way help to restore the central place of the family and norms of marital fidelity and family stability—which are at the very core of a sound culture—spouses should simply take their marriage vows seriously, and work to be the best spouses and parents that they can be. It appears, by the way, that a certain, significant element in the U.S. is now doing that, the upper middle class and well-off elements clustered in the high-end suburban enclaves that Charles Murray discusses in his book *Coming Apart: The State of White America, 1960-2010* (even though Murray says "they don't preach what they practice").[18]

Those of a more intellectual cast should rightfully plan to "go deeper." College students should seek out sound professors (i.e., who have a good formation, are not taken with political correctness, and are committed to the principles of the Founding and the cultural traditions behind them) and take pertinent courses (e.g., history, political science, literature) from them whenever possible. They should take courses wherever possible that will enable them to read the Great Books. Such professors, or even the students themselves, can form the kinds of informal study groups, with a more academic cast perhaps, that were mentioned above to enable college students to learn about sound philosophy, the Western cultural heritage, and the Constitution when formal courses are not available. As future leaders in American political society in the public and private sectors, college students could do no better than focus some of their informal study attention on Alexis de Tocqueville—whose *Democracy in America* (1835-1840) is arguably still the most insightful work on the nature of American culture—if they cannot find actual college courses that give attention to his thought. They can take advantage of the (often free) programs of the Intercollegiate Studies Institute—whose specific mission is to aid in the intellectual formation of college students to better understand many of the very principles and traditions we are concerned about—and related groups.

Professors like these and other solid professionals could form speakers bureaus in local communities and make themselves available—as a free, public-spirited service—to citizen groups and other institutions to speak on different aspects of the Western cultural tradition, the Constitution, the Founding Fathers, the ideas of the Founding, etc. They can work with interested local businessmen and other concerned citizens to restore the great American Revolutionary Era tradition of pamphleteering in order to re-educate their fellow citizens about, say the principles of America's Founding, and can simply do things like showing up at parades and public events on national holidays to distribute them, make them available on library public information racks, leave them in places where free literature can be picked up, etc. With the financial help of businessmen, they could mail them, say, to the people listed on selected pages in local phone books (maybe even a few very wealthy national business leaders could be convinced to help bankroll a larger effort). They can offer free adult education and informal courses for college and high school students on basic logic and reasoning correctly and basic principles of realist philosophy, since as stated the root of the present-day cultural crisis is the abandonment of reason.

As was stated above, people—everyday people or the more intellectually inclined—who understand the importance of the principles of the Western cultural heritage and the American political tradition should commit themselves to openly, forthrightly, and courageously—but also kindly and patiently—defending them to others. A small amount of courage, by many people day in and day out, can have significant results, and showing that truth can be spoken in the spirit of love of neighbor can go a long way toward promoting civility. This can be a ready witness that—contrary to the church-state separationists and moral relativists—insisting that there are truths that must control our public and communal life does not inevitably bring intolerance and oppression in its wake.

One other important effort needs to start at the inter-personal level. It must start there so it can then continue at other levels. This is the need to recover language. As Rita Marker, one of the founders of Franciscan University of Steubenville's Human Life Studies Program, Executive Director of the Patients Rights Council, and an internationally known opponent of euthanasia, would always say, "verbal engineering precedes social engineering." We can't concede the prerogative of shaping the terminology to the adversaries of sound culture. It was not a mistake that the homosexualist movement appropriated the term "gay." They were trying to convey that same-sex attraction and, in fact, sodomy were not just normal but positive and benevolent. Indeed, we should not even have conceded something as basic as the rejection of the use of the masculine generic—"he" or "his"—and accept the supposedly "inclusive" practice of saying "he or she" and "his or her." This, and the entire feminist-inspired language upheaval, did not occur because of a need to treat males and females equally—there was never a question that right-thinking people understood men and women to be equal in the correct sense of the word—but arguably because it provided a linguistic underpinning for the feminist revolution and later the homosexualist revolution in obliterating gender differences.

Citizen action, especially against the overreaching of government, has to be carried out not just on the individual level but also must feature mass action. I am not talking about civil disobedience, but about perfectly legal rallies, marches, and demonstrations.[19] Along these lines, the approach of the early TEA Party movement to have large demonstrations in Washington, D.C. and elsewhere before—erroneously, in my opinion—turning their attention mostly to primary challenges in the Republican party is a good paradigm. While the TEA Party's effort has mostly been on fiscal-related issues, citizen groups should consider this kind of strategy for many other public issues as well.

Restoring the family is certainly an essential element of cultural renewal. We can be stymied in this effort, however, if we first cannot protect the family. One of the main governmental assaults on it—widespread but long under the radar screen, at least until such dramatic developments as the Justina Pelletier case—has been carried out by the so-called "child protective system" (CPS). The CPS was brought into existence supposedly to combat child abuse and neglect, but in fact only a small minority of the reports it investigates concern true abuse or neglect. We don't have an epidemic of child abuse/neglect, but an epidemic of false reporting of it. As I have discussed in a series of lengthy scholarly articles over a quarter-century,[20] the CPS routinely interferes with legitimate parental actions and subverts parental rights. It is a fundamentally coercive, totalitarian-like system that features in theory, at least, an almost universal monitoring of parents and their child-rearing practices. It presents an area that calls out for vigorous, visible citizen action along TEA Party lines. I suspect that if there were organized, active parents' and related citizen's groups that regularly picketed and called press conferences at county courthouses and CPS agencies (the CPS across the country is organized mostly on the county level with an overarching state agency above it) to call attention to the its systemic abuses and major periodic "protect-the-family" rallies or something like that in state capitals, coupled with the ongoing legal efforts in defense of parental rights by organizations like the Home School Legal Defense Association and Family Defense Center in Chicago, it would not be too long before there would be major changes in the CPS. The effectiveness of direct, mass citizen action was seen dramatically in France in the 1980s when to oppose government initiatives to put more restraints on Catholic and other private education, a million people took part in a massive rally—most of whom probably were not drawn from the sector of French political society most accustomed to public protesting—and the government beat a hasty retreat.[21]

There is another dimension of citizen action that is important. Part of what the renewal of culture involves is for people to begin to try to break free from the control of distant entities, whether private or governmental—that is, to work to give substance to a central principle of social ethics, subsidiarity. Citizen efforts need to be undertaken, on the one hand, to help insure that human needs are addressed and on the other to enable people to gain greater control over their economic destiny. Families need to refocus their thinking on caring for their own, to doing what Pope St. John Paul II called for in his striking critique of the "social assistance" state in the encyclical *Centesimus Annus*: to take responsibility for helping those in need at that level as much as possible.[22] To assist the family with this, when needed, we need to set our minds on the building up of a healthy, vigorous, and somewhat transformed "civil society" sector. Citizens shouldn't wait for or concede responsibility to the established, often large, entities in that sector—many of which are partially funded by government. What they can do is to devote themselves more to sustained volunteer efforts and working to build up intermediate groups to help each other in this regard.

While it would be unrealistic—and maybe disadvantageous—for people to think they could simply turn their backs on large-scale economic enterprises, what they can do—if they have the interest, talents, and wherewithal—is to think anew about working to build more small-scale enterprises and cottage industries. Some of these things could be cooperative endeavors, and that itself could have the added advantage of helping to rebuild community that has been so weakened in an era of mass culture. If such things could catch on, over an extended period of time people might begin to see that the American populace does not have to be a simple victim, without any recourse at all, of global economic trends and that government is not the only or best entity to help them. A few examples might be expanded cooperative efforts of various kinds among small businesses in the same field—perhaps along the lines of some types of rural cooperatives—the organizations set up by certain groups of Christians to pool funds to help each other with health care expenses, and the special clinics set up by some physicians that offer a full range of health care services to people without insurance for a low flat monthly "membership-type" fee. These are modest efforts, but if enough such things were put in place and proven to be successful, it could gradually shift people's attention toward a more small-scale, localized, non-governmental approach to social welfare and, to some extent (especially if more people are also working to restrain their runaway demand for material possessions), economic activity. This would be like the conditions that prevailed in the culture of the American Founding Era, and would help to reignite such admirable cultural norms of that period as industry, overcoming adversity, honesty and fair-dealing, commercial efficiency, a spirit of independence, and a willingness to make present sacrifices for expected future good.[23] To be sure, prevailing law may be an obstacle to some of these citizen initiatives (e.g., in the health care area). Citizen organizations and small businesses have to be as aggressive as possible in resisting, politically and legally, governmental efforts to over-regulate and regiment them and stop them from undertaking the kind of initiatives just mentioned. Where people *have* to rely on larger, more distant economic entities, concerted citizen action should be used to restrain their excesses, especially their attempts to further deleterious cultural trends. For example, people resisting the secular culture should organize letter campaigns and well-chosen, well-thought-out, focused boycotts against large companies that have "signed on" to the homosexualist agenda. Conversely, they should openly and pronouncedly support companies that have resisted such trends, like the support shown to Chick-fil-A a few years ago.[24]

Legal Efforts

To let the above kinds of individual and family efforts have the time to build up a better culture, legal and political efforts are necessary to enable us to have the freedom to do them. I have already mentioned about legal advocacy organizations working for parental rights. On the religious liberty front we have seen the indispensable work of such organizations as the Alliance Defending Freedom, the Thomas More Law Center, and the Becket Fund in coming to the aid of ordinary citizens, small businesses, and churches that have been threatened by government as it tries to impose the tenets of a secular public philosophy and morality. Lawyers who recognize the dangers need to step up in larger numbers to join small-government, public interest legal advocacy organizations or simply act on their own to offer free or low-cost voluntary legal help to such citizens and groups. I have written that something more is needed than legal defense, however. The struggle against the formidable forces of the secular culture cannot succeed in this respect or in others if those engaged in it do not go on the offensive—more, they must be *consistently* on the offensive. Legal efforts are needed that will pursue actions in tort and other areas of the law against officials and organizations who trample on religious liberty, free speech, and other constitutional rights. Homosexualist organizations and activists who have gone after the Christians who won't do things like provide services for same-sex "weddings" or who have pushed for the ouster of corporate officials who supported pro-true marriage efforts and the like should be held to account legally for these actions. If they were to see their resources depleted having to defend legitimate tort actions, they would likely back off of what they are doing. Civil rights law, labor and employment law, and even traditional principles of contract law should be used to call companies to task when they accede to such homosexualist demands.[25] Resuscitating the seldom-used tort action of abuse of process would cause outfits like the Freedom from Religion Foundation (FFRF) to be much more restrained in their efforts to impose almost a fanatical secularism on American life. Maybe if local officials—the typical target of the FFRF—saw that skilled, volunteer lawyers are ready with a response like this they would be less likely to just surrender to their threats.

Even this expanded effort at legal advocacy is not sufficient, however. Those in the pro-traditional culture legal community must also make use of every opportunity to educate both the public and their colleagues in law about what are our traditional common law and constitutional principles and liberties, and show how central they were to our Founding background. They must also show how the claimed "rights" and legal perspectives of the secular culture—like same-sex "marriage" and the twisted notion of equality used to justify it—are without basis in our legal tradition and why they hold the prospect of undoing it.

The Kinds of Political Responses that Should Be Considered

If the efforts on the personal and family level for cultural renewal and to try to influence public decision-making are mostly modest, some of what I have suggested—especially in my columns and some of my other writing—to be aimed for at the political level are, to be sure, large objectives. Nevertheless, they are increasingly important ones to be thinking about and are possible under the right circumstances.

First, the question comes up as to how Christian and other political candidates who are truly concerned about taking on and changing the secular culture should go about doing it. This is really a broader question about what kind of politics is needed in an age of cultural meltdown. I reiterate here what I said about this in one of my columns.[26] As with the other levels at which the secular culture has to be challenged, in the political arena there must be a combination of courage, insistence, unremitting assertiveness (an offensive posture, a true political saviness), and an educative approach. That is, the long-lost educative function of politics cries out to be rediscovered. The prime focus of the serious Christian politician cannot be concern about the next election; the stakes are simply too high now. As I said in my column, immediate electoral success accomplishes little if the Republic and the culture are in shambles.

The recovery of the crucial educative function of politics requires having a sound substantive understanding of the questions of the day and also mastering rhetoric (in the best sense of the word). The old expression, "it's not what you say but how you say it," is pertinent here. The political left and the other apologists of the secular culture should not be permitted, as is so often the case, to define the terms of the debate. To effectively carry out the educative function of politics, one has to first create the conditions that make it possible, to clear out the obstacles to it. What this means, among other things, is that one has to "call out" the secular left. A Christian politician must show, persistently and emphatically, how the left's agenda and objectives have become increasingly irrational and explain how potentially destructive they are. Further, he should show how they use manipulation, deception, and untruth to promote it and not hesitate to show the opportunism that's often involved (e.g., how politicians who were once against abortion and same-sex "marriage" changed course, without any sense of principle, when the political winds did). Christian politicians should not hold back because of a supposed concern about being uncharitable. The maxim for Christians has always been, "speak the truth in love." Too often, however, Christians in our time confuse charity with a kind of sentimentalism bred by the nonjudgmental ethos that is rife in the secular culture. Truth ends up being the casualty. I remember a prayer booklet I once had that stated the different kinds of demands that Christianity puts on its adherents. One of these was "toward the evil, it is *resistance*" (emphasis added).

Christians in public life, by the way, should also not be reluctant to put the media enablers of their secular leftist opponents on the hot seat when the occasion presents itself. They need to cultivate a genuine astuteness in dealing with the media. Instead of answering just the questions that the media asks them or letting the media put them on the defensive or set obvious snares for them, they should be sure to be a step or two ahead of them. They need to anticipate the media's questions and angles and make sure, again, to be careful of their language and be in control rhetorically. They should also not be hesitant to point out to the media where their understanding of something is incorrect—this, too, is part of the educative function of politics—or to challenge their opportunism every bit as much as they do that of their opponents. For example, when Clintonista George Stephanopoulos pulled the contraception issue out of the hat in the Republican debates of 2012—apparently to set up the "war on women" issue—the candidates should have repeatedly hammered him for the rest of the debate for his manipulation of facts, unfairness, and for misusing his journalistic position to assist Obama and the Democratic party.

How a Christian political candidate or, say, legislator concerned about cultural renewal should put this approach into practice can be illustrated with the issues of abortion in "hard" cases and same-sex "marriage." One can recall the situation of Representative Todd Akin in the 2012 U.S. Senate campaign in Missouri when he clumsily answered a journalist's gotcha question about abortion in the case of rape. It also points to what is the best way to deal with the issue of abortion for "hard cases." Besides stressing the small percentage of abortions sought as a result of rape[27] (which is usually a false issue raised by people supporting abortion on demand), a pro-life candidate should "call out" the inquisitor, accusing him openly of insincerity: it's a gotcha question with, simply stated, a pro-abortion agenda. The best way to argue against abortion here and in all cases, of course, is to focus *repeatedly* on the conclusive facts about the unborn child's humanity—regardless the circumstances of his conception. The aim should be to put and keep pro-abortionists on the defensive and hold the rhetorical higher ground—provide the truth and, more, *keep pounding it home.* As important as sound arguments are, however, many people need to be touched personally. So Christian, pro-life candidates could do no better than to occasionally have pro-life speakers who were conceived in rape but whose mothers chose life—or abortion survivors or just women who have suffered physically or psychologically from abortions—join them on the campaign trail.

Finally, how do pro-family candidates tackle same-sex "marriage"? This is actually harder, given the now deep-seated convoluted thinking about rights and equality. Rights are now viewed as essentially grounded in desires—personal preferences—that should prevail as long as someone is not obviously hurt by their exercise. Equality means that everyone should be able to exercise the same rights. Isn't that just fair? Our individualistic ethos also makes contemporary Americans unable to recognize damage to the social fabric and how that ultimately can hurt people. Since people need to hear about harms, candidates cannot go easy on active homosexuals; there is no way to oppose same-sex "marriage" without targeting sodomy. So, the significant health consequences of homosexual practices must be repeatedly emphasized,[28] as must the fact that their being allowed to "marry" will not (as some claim) check their tendency to have multiple sexual partners.[29] The obvious harm of that for any children present—who were, say, adopted or from IVF or a previous heterosexual relationship or marriage—must be underscored. The emerging evidence, anecdotal and from studies, of the range of deleterious effects generally on children reared in same-sex households must repeatedly be pointed to.[30] Still, with the aggressive efforts of the homosexualist movement to debunk even the soundest research, Christian pro-family candidates have to take the educative function of politics to a deeper level. That means not being afraid to talk about what marriage and the family are supposed to be, why they can't be merely or fundamentally an exercise in individual desire or predilection, why marriage cannot be closed off from procreation and childrearing, and why it has to be seen as an enduring association. They have to explain the dangers of allowing it to be redefined or defined in any way someone wants to for individuals—especially children (and there is now plenty of evidence about the long-term effects of family breakdown on the rising generation)—and our culture and political life. To counter the drumbeat for same-sex "marriage," they probably will even have to speak about another almost verboten topic of recent decades: how men and women actually are different and why children need both. While we can't expect politicians truly to be moral and religious teachers, we are in a time where Christian politicians have to play an important role in educating the public about the moral and practical problems of the wayward cultural norms and practices that have taken hold. When it comes to the homosexualist movement and, more broadly, the entire sexual-libertine left, Christian politicians should consistently attack their increasingly repressive and, in fact, totalitarian tendencies (which is seen, *inter alia*, in the forcing of bakers and events planners to take part in same-sex "weddings," the banning of reparative therapy for minors to change same-sex attraction, the pressures to topple opponents of same-sex "marriage" from corporate positions, the HHS mandate on contraceptives and abortifacients, and in the diminishing of conscience protections for health-care workers). Again, the educational effort must be combined with a confrontational stance that aims to put the proponents of destructive cultural transformation on the defensive.

This is a new kind of politics, to be sure, but one necessary to rescue a collapsing culture. It is also not one that can readily be dismissed as an electoral loser. It may take extra time for the message to sink in, but if done correctly—with a combination of an offensive posture, persistence, education, astutely anticipating the opposition, mastering rhetoric, and a charitable spirit—I believe it can have the effect sought. Let's keep in mind that our current "politics as usual" politicians, who may understand the need to address our cultural problems but can't see beyond short-term electoral success, often succeed at neither.

Further, Christian politicians trying to change the culture need to be willing to go against the grain, at least to some degree, when in office. It is easy, for example, when elected to Congress to buy into the Beltway mentality and to think just about perpetuating oneself in office. They need to be prepared to embrace ideas that do not fit into the comfortable pattern and be prepared to take initiatives even if their party leadership does not support them. We have the unfortunate situation now where one of our political parties has moved more toward the doctrinaire left and embraced many culturally corrosive forces, and the other one, despite opposing this, basically maintains a holding pattern when it takes power. The result is that nothing is achieved and the culture just gets worse.

What I have argued for some time is that executive power may be especially crucial at least to upholding and, in fact, in many respects restoring American constitutional principles and especially protect traditional citizen rights at a time when they are under increasingly relentless attack.[31] On the other hand, one cannot expect executive leadership to rebuild our crumbling culture. That is beyond what any one man can do. A solid president can have a salutary effect, however. Even while we are witnessing a misuse and possibly unconstitutional use of executive power in the Obama Presidency, we should not shy away from the strong, even sweeping use—although within the Constitution and our traditions—of executive power to help rescue us.

Let us consider the historical justification for very strong executive power in times such as ours. In ancient Greece and Rome, in times of great internal turmoil or external threat, there was provision for giving almost absolute power to an eminent, trustworthy man to get them out of the mess. So, when the Athenians got into trouble they turned to the great ethical poet Solon and gave him near complete power. He made sweeping but wise reforms that ameliorated the tensions among classes that were threatening to break out into civil war. After the crisis passed, he stepped down and went into self-imposed exile.[32] The senate in early republican Rome twice made the statesman and former military leader Lucius Quinctius Cincinnatus dictator (that term then did not have the pejorative connotation that it does now), once to battle enemy tribes that were about to swarm over the city and later to defeat an internal conspiracy. He assumed power just long enough to do his job, and then returned to the plow on his farm.[33] Both men were notable examples of self-limited power to our Founding Fathers. George Washington was sometimes called the "American Cincinnatus."[34]

Both Aristotle and John Locke said that in times of a breakdown in sound culture and the rule of law—both of which we are witnessing today—executive power assumes greater importance. While Locke was the great promoter of parliamentary power against kingly absolutism, he nevertheless endorsed "prerogative power." This gave the political executive the discretion to act for the public good "without the prescription of law and sometimes even against it."[35] Actually, what's needed right now in America is not really for the president to act outside the law, but to exert extraordinary power to *uphold our fundamental law*, the Constitution, and the principles of our tradition and the natural law that stand behind it. Edward S. Corwin, perhaps the greatest American constitutional scholar of the first half of the twentieth century, said that our Founders believed that "a broad range of autonomous executive power or 'prerogative'" was lodged in the presidency. He also emphasized that such power was not limited to wartime or even to situations of great urgency, but could be exercised so long as needed for the "public good."[36] Theodore Roosevelt's "stewardship" theory of the presidency embraced a similar perspective.[37] In his book, *Constitutional Dictatorship*, the famous historian Clinton Rossiter showed how contemporary constitutional regimes have found it necessary in times of crisis to grant extraordinary power to government, especially executives, that for a time may even to some degree alter the character of the regime.[38]

What is needed now is not necessarily the extra-constitutional means that Lincoln used to save the Constitution, but rather the utilization of powers that presidents possess but have seldom exercised or exercised to the degree necessary. While we are not witnessing wholesale disorder of the nature of, say, widespread violence in the streets—though the racial clashes of 2014 and 2015 are localized examples of that and we certainly see massive amounts of more specific violence, as in abortion—we are certainly facing a deeper, cultural disorder that becomes more intense each passing year.

A new American Cincinnatus—a president who would exercise executive power to perhaps an unprecedented degree—could certainly act forcefully and decisively to protect traditional citizen liberties when the courts do not or when they themselves thwart them. In truly serious situations, he could refuse to enforce outrageous, unconstitutional court decisions and even resist them when necessary. He could act to insure that true American constitutional principles will be upheld. As I said, rebuilding a sound culture is not something one man can do alone, but he could take dramatic initiatives—even if resisted by the other branches—that could decisively set the country in that direction. In the long run, or even sometimes the short run, people will fall in line and accept a new course that a leader insistently sets them on, even if they resist it at the start. This would especially be so if he led the way in reviving the educative function of politics, persistently making his case to the public in an understandable way while always remaining on the rhetorical offensive against his opposition and not allowing himself to be outflanked by it.

There are many specific things that he should do: reverse Obama's executive orders; sweepingly abrogate federal regulatory law in many areas—starting with the HHS mandate, EPA overreaches, and a whole host of repressive IRS regulations—and simultaneously act vigorously to get the kind of control over the federal bureaucracy that presidents are supposed to have; put the federal government on a firm course of gradual disengagement from many programmatic areas by refusing to seek reauthorizations and progressively cutting down the federal budget (while at the same time making sure the human needs in question are addressed by actively working to build up civil society); interpose federal power to protect churches and defend religious and personal liberty against the encroachments of state agencies, such as when human relations commissions force Christians to violate their consciences by providing services for same-sex "weddings" and states subvert parents' rights to make choices about medical care for their children (as with the aforementioned reparative therapy for same-sex inclined children and Justina Pelletier-like "medical kidnapping" cases); even more critically, he could intervene with federal power—irrespective of what the courts say—to protect the Terri Schiavos of the future; he could outright refuse to carry out unconstitutional Supreme Court decisions such as *U.S. v. Windsor*, which mandated that federal benefits be given to same-sex "spouses"[39] and block decisions that try to further remove religion from the public domain; take an aggressive stance against the UN and EU as they try to subvert authentic human rights in favor of the homosexualist and sexual libertine agenda; and, perhaps most dramatically, finally engineer a constitutional confrontation against the Court on abortion. If, say, a state governor rounded up every member of a certain ethnic group and put them in a concentration camp, would anyone seriously say that the president has no power to stop it if a federal court refused to do so? It is no different with abortion: a whole class of American citizens is summarily being deprived of a right even more fundamental than their liberty, their life. So, would a president truly be acting tyrannically by simply shutting down the abortion clinics? If rebuking the Supreme Court seems extreme or unthinkable, we should recall: Federalist 78, which says that *only* the executive has the sword (that is, the enforcement power)[40]; Andrew Jackson's refusal to carry out the Court's mandate in the *Cherokee Indian Cases* (which rendered it null)[41]; and Lincoln's insistence that a Supreme Court decision, such as *Dred Scott*, did not bind the political branches for all time.[42] If it's true that the president—and Congress, for that matter—may not resist the most blatantly unconstitutional decisions by the courts, we have become what Russell Kirk called an "archonocracy" instead of a democratic republic.[43]

Executive power used in even an unprecedented way does not mean despotism. Rather, when exercised by a virtuous, capable man with a strong sense of self-limitation and an understanding that it is only temporary, it can be used to *stop* the slide to despotism. Building up a healthy culture and political order take much time, but if we don't check—more, start to reverse—the advanced state of decay of our traditional liberties and constitutional principles, we may not get the chance. In ordinary times, we can accept the interminable deliberation, plodding, excessive compromising, and willy-nilly decision-making of legislative bodies. It is different in times of crisis, where a civilization hangs in the balance and time is short. We can't even seem to forge legislative majorities that will uphold our traditions and moral truth. This is even apart from what was said above about how even though many politicians go to Washington committed to stopping the dangerous socio-politico-cultural trends of the time, no significant initiatives almost ever seem to be taken to do that.

The challenge obviously is how to bring forth and get the new American Cincinnatus elected. I don't have an answer to that, except to say that Christians and others seeking in a serious way to confront the secular culture and protect American traditions should look to executive power—rightly exercised by a thoroughly moral, self-limited, and capable man—to lead the way, and as they evaluate prospective presidential candidates, should consider who can best be trusted to exercise power at least somewhat in this manner and be effective at it.

As I wrote in another of my columns, we can also look to state governors to provide strong executive leadership to help check the erosion of traditional rights—even if the influence they can have, even in their own states, is much less than with a president. We saw this when Maine Governor Paul LaPage ordered state child welfare bureaucrats—who are under his authority—to agree to a mother's wish to cancel a DNR order for her badly injured, hospitalized baby despite the medical authorities' wish to keep it in place.[44] He did this despite the bureaucrats' getting a court order to back them up. He even threatened to defy the Maine Supreme Judicial Court if it upheld the lower court (as it turned out, the Supreme Judicial Court said the case was moot after the state bureaucrats dropped their demand).[45] The rights of Justina Pelletier and her parents could similarly have been protected from an out-of-control state child protective system if Massachusetts had had a similar-type governor.

The Catholic Church in America and the Challenge to the Secular Culture

I will add a few final remarks about the Church's stance in the U.S. against the secular culture. While I cannot go much into this—it is the topic of an entire book—I have to make a few observations, especially in light of recent troubling developments. These include (these are only a few examples): one high-ranking American prelate who seems to have embraced homosexualist "identity politics" in commending a prominent athlete for "coming out" about his same-sex attraction and also saying that the issue of withholding Holy Communion from pro-abortion politicians is in the past,[46] and another high-ranking prelate seeming to agree[47]; the former editor of a prominent religious journal of opinion, which tilts Catholic, and is a "conservative" Catholic himself endorsing same-sex "marriage"[48]; and the St. Patrick's Day parades in New York City and Boston opening themselves up to homosexualist groups marching in them, apparently without objection from the institutional Church.[49] One wonders if these developments are not signaling a number of things: a sense that certain unfortunate things have just become the norm and we'll have to just cut our losses and work with them and do the best we can; a belief that there has to be a *rapproachment* with the secular culture because of a belief that civility (in some sense of the word) requires it; a misguided pastoral concern that—while not dissenting from Church teaching—holds that certain doctrinal issues can be glossed over for now (and maybe that we can get back to them later) or at least that the Church would do better to focus on evangelization and not address moral issues in the public sphere (as if that were not part of evangelization);[50] a weariness—a feeling of being "punch-drunk"—in the ongoing, seemingly interminable, culture wars; and a belief—that one of the aforementioned high-ranking American prelates has emphasized—that what we really need in the "culture wars" is more dialogue, with the implicit assumption that the adversaries are willing to listen.[51]

I am skeptical, to say the least, about all of these points. I have said consistently in this paper that a mixture of an offensive posture and education is needed to challenge the secular culture and those who are trying to uphold it and its many manifestations. In other words, there is no problem about dialoguing, but we cannot do just that and we cannot do it on the adversary's terms. There is always a danger in not emphasizing strongly enough—in an "up-front" manner—the truth. Nor can we be too optimistic about the adversary's willingness to listen. As the eminent Catholic social scientist Msgr. Paul Hanly Furfey said in the middle decades of the twentieth century, the attempt to reach out to unbelievers in a manner which glosses over any parts of Catholic doctrine has been fruitless in bringing them around to see the wisdom of Catholicism, and has often "been a prolific source of dogmatic error" in the Church.[52] I also suggested in one of my columns that perhaps some Catholic leaders are falling prey to the temptation to confuse charity with a false notion of compassion characteristic itself of the secular culture.[53] They may also have bought into the secular culture's erroneous view alluded to above—and seen so vividly in the Supreme Court's perspective about religious establishment—that civility requires the downplaying of at least the most unpopular truths. While I acknowledge that there are high obstacles to overcome to renew the culture and am aware that the building of a culture usually takes a very long time, I think we should not fall into the trap of viewing the task as insurmountable or thinking that the current secular culture is more impregnable than it really is and that its various accoutrements more engrained than they truly are.

As I said in a column, if some in the U.S. Catholic leadership are allowing themselves to be crippled—and, unwittingly, perhaps weakening the Christian witness—then the laity who understand the problem have to—perhaps more than ever before—step up to the plate.[54] It is time to understand what perhaps American Catholics—both clerical and lay—historically have never quite fully gotten down: the role of the laity is to take the lead in the realm of affairs, that is the true domain of the laity. A properly formed and informed laity has to take the initiative to challenge the secular culture and try to change it, they have to do the work of reforming—that is, *re-forming*—it in the social, political, economic, legal, and institutional realms. The American laity at last has to realize that it cannot wait for the bishops, clergy, or Church bureaucracies to do this. To be sure, if their bishops and clergy are not viewing the problems of culture and public life correctly they should also express their dissatisfaction—and try to educate them in a spirit of charity and humility.

There is one other thing that the Catholic laity should turn its attention to, especially since we are talking about how to deal with the secular culture. The laity should consider, with appropriate direction by clergy who share their commitment to cultural change, how it can increasingly and in an organized fashion engage in apologetic efforts.[55] The Catholic laity may even be able to work, to some degree, with laity of other Christian churches that are truly faithful to the tradition, to make the case for Christ in an age of unbelief. After all, at the most basic level when we think about challenging and changing a secular culture we are talking about conversion.

I close by returning to the question of the seeming insurmountability of the task. I recall occasionally for my students how those of us who lived through the Cold War believed that the division between East and West was a permanent feature of our international life—then all of a sudden, even though it was not foreseeable five or even perhaps two years before, communism collapsed. More, it crumbled not with the worldwide cataclysm that so many feared, but almost with a whimper. At bottom line, communism fell because of the same fundamental problem as today's secular culture in the West: it was on a collision course with human nature—what I said at the beginning of this paper. The collapse of communism didn't happen automatically, however. Besides prayer—my teacher Fr. Robert Levis of EWTN fame told me at the time that this was the fruit of little old ladies praying the rosary for seventy years since 1917—forty-five years of Western opposition (at various degrees of intensity) and the ongoing courageous witness of so many dissidents in Communist countries, the decade immediately before the collapse featured the "Eastern policy" of Pope St. John Paul II and the determined efforts of President Ronald Reagan who believed against all prevailing wisdom—even among the foreign policy experts—that change could occur in the Soviet Bloc and that the U.S. should do whatever it could to encourage it.[56] There was also the *collaboration* between these two epochal men to make this happen—a story that still hasn't fully been told. There was also something else: the decline of the hold of the Communist ideology.[57] This parallels the condition of Western secular culture, mentioned above, where the dissolution of all certitudes and the sole remaining ethic of autonomy inches us ever closer to outright nihilism—and what has come along with this, as Pope Francis has suggested, is a lot of personal suffering, hurt, and pain. The conditions may cry out for a restoration of sound culture much sooner than we imagine.

Notes

[1] Stephen M. Krason, *The Transformation of the American Democratic Republic* (Piscataway, N.J.: Transaction, 2012), 498. See, generally, the discussion in Chaps. 1 and 10.

[2] Americo Lapati, "Orestes A. Brownson: American Catholic Political Thinker (1806-1873), in Stephen M. Krason, ed., *Catholic Makers of America: Biographical Sketches of Catholic Statesmen and Political Thinkers in America's First Century, 1776-1876* (Front Royal, VA: Christendom Press, 1993), 182.

[3] See "How Human Rights Are Becoming 'Post and Trans-Human Rights,'" translation of an interview published originally in French by Flora Thomasset, *La Croix*, Friday October 31, 2014, 11.

[4] 505 U.S. 833, 851.

[5] "How Human Rights Are Becoming 'Post and Trans-Human Rights.'"

[6] See Robert P. George, *Making Men Moral: Civil Liberties and Public Morality* (Oxford: Oxford University Press, 1993).

[7] Most of my discussion that follows in this section appears—in close to the same wording—in *The Transformation of the American Democratic Republic*, 491-496.

[8] *The Transformation of the American Democratic Republic*, 490.

[9] Allan Bloom, *The Closing of the American Mind: How Higher Education Has Failed Democracy and Impoverished the Souls of Today's Students* (N.Y.: Simon & Schuster [Touchstone]), 1987), 344-347. David Lowenthal, who is a fellow follower of Bloom's of the great twentieth-century scholar of political philosophy, Leo Strauss, says much the same thing. See Lowenthal, "Liberal Education: Originally and Today," in Stephen M. Krason, ed., *The Recovery of American Education: Reclaiming a Vision*, (Lanham, Md.: University Press of America, 1991), 73.

[10] William J. Bennett, *The Book of Virtues: A Treasury of Great Moral Stories* (N.Y.: Simon and Schuster, 1993).

[11] See, e.g.: "Academic Statistics on Homeschooling," http://www.hslda.org/docs/nche/000010/200410250.asp; Internet; accessed 4 July 2010.

[12] Pope John Paul II, "Peace With God the Creator, Peace With All of Creation" (World Day of Peace Statement, Dec. 8, 1989), sec. IV; Pope John Paul II, *Centesimus Annus* (*The Hundredth Year*), #58.

[13] See *The Transformation of the American Democratic Republic*, 492-493.

[14] It is a basic teaching of the Catholic Church that men do not keep the natural law for long without God's help—that is, without religion (Sacred Congregation for the Clergy, *General Catechetical Directory*, #61).

[15] See *The Transformation of the American Democratic Republic*, 11-15.

[16] In *The Transformation of the American Democratic Republic* (21-22), I discuss several prominent thinkers who address the problem of the cultural/civilizational decline or the decline of political orders.

[17] See Krason, *The Transformation of the American Democratic Republic*, 15-18, 22.

[18] Charles Murray, *Coming Apart: The State of White America, 1960-2010* (N.Y.: Crown Forum, 2012), 295, 305.

[19] I have argued for a long time against civil disobedience as a tactic for the pro-life movement for an assortment of reasons (see Stephen M. Krason, *The Public Order and the Sacred Order: Contemporary Issues, Catholic Social Thought, and the Western and American Traditions* (Lanham, MD: Scarecrow Press, 2009), chap. 7.

[20] See: "Child Abuse: Pseudo-Crisis, Dangerous Bureaucrats, Destroyed Families," in Stephen M. Krason & Robert J. D'Agostino, eds., *Parental Rights: The Contemporary Assault on Traditional Liberties* (Front Royal, Va.: Christendom College Press, 1988); "A Grave Threat to the Family: American Law and Public Policy on Child Abuse and Neglect," in Paul C. Vitz and Stephen M. Krason, eds., *Defending the Family: A Sourcebook* (Steubenville, O.: Catholic Social Science Press, 1998); "Child Abuse and Neglect: Failed Policy and Assault on Innocent Parents," in *The Catholic Social Science Review*, vol. X (2005); "The Critics of the Current Child Abuse Laws and the Child Protective System: A Survey of the Leading Literature," in *The Catholic Social Science Review*, vol. XII (2007); and "The Mondale Act and Its Aftermath: An Overview of Forty Years of American Law, Public Policy, and Governmental Response to Child Abuse and Neglect," in Stephen M. Krason, ed., *Child Abuse, Family Rights, and the Child Protective System: A Critical Analysis from Law, Ethics, and Catholic Social Teaching* (Lanham, Md.: Scarecrow Press, 2013), 1-81.

[21] See "Jean-Marie Lustiger," http://en.wikipedia.org/wiki/Jean-Marie_Lustiger; Internet; "Alain Savary," http://en.wikipedia.org/wiki/Alain_Savary; Internet; both accessed 11 June 2010.

[22] *Centesimus Annus*, #48-49.

[23] See *The Transformation of the American Democratic Republic*, 16.

[24] In 2012, Chick-fil-A's CEO made a number of public statements supporting true marriage, between a man and a woman. Same-sex "marriage" activists began a boycott of the restaurant chain. In response, Mike Huckabee, former governor of Arkansas and presidential candidate who then had a program on Fox News, called for a Chick-fil-A Appreciation Day and public responded with massive support for the company including record-breaking sales on that day (see: https://en.wikipedia.org/wiki/Chick-fil-A#Same-sex_marriage_controversy).

[25] These kinds of legal efforts and counter-efforts seem even more crucial in light of the likelihood of enhanced legal bullying of conscientious objectors by government agencies and homosexualist organizations in the aftermath of the U.S. Supreme Court's *Obergefell v. Hodges* decision of 2015 (576 U.S.____) declaring same-sex "marriage" a constitutional right, which was handed down as this book was being prepared for publication.

[26] The material in the next several paragraphs, up to the discussion of executive power, largely comes from my column, "Presidential Power: A Rescuer, Not a Nemesis," in *Crisismagazine.com* (March 10, 2014).

[27] See Stephen M. Krason, *Abortion: Politics, Morality, and the Constitution: A Critical Study of* Roe v. Wade *and* Doe v. Bolton *and a Basis for Change* (Lanham, Md.: University Press of America, 1984), 281-283.

[28] See, e.g., Peter Sprigg & Timothy Dailey, eds., *Getting It Straight: What the Research Shows about Homosexuality* (Washington, D.C.: Family Research Council, 2004), 69-93.

[29] See Peter Sprigg, "The Top Ten Harms of Same-Sex 'Marriage'" (brochure), 4-5; http://www.frc.org/brochure/the-top-ten-harms-of-same-sex-marriage; Internet; accessed 2 May 2015.

[30] See Peter Sprigg, "New Study on Homosexual Parents Tops All Previous Research," http://www.frc.org/issuebrief/new-study-on-homosexual-parents-tops-all-previous-research; Internet; accessed 2 May 2015. The study referred to is reported in the following article: Mark Regnerus, "How Different Are the Adult Children of Parents Who Have Same-Sex Relationships? Findings from the New Family Structures Study," *Social Science Research*, vol. 41, no. 4 (July 2012), 752-770.

[31] I most recently wrote about this in two of my columns in *Crisismagazine.com*: "Presidential Power: A Rescuer, Not a Nemesis" (March 10, 2014) and "More on Presidential Power as Rescuer: A Rejoinder," (April 11, 2014). I have also written two longer scholarly articles on this topic: "The New Recourse to Executive Power: Weapon of the Culture Wars," *The Public Order and the Sacred Order*, 565-572, and "Executive Authority," in M. Coulter, S. Krason, R. Myers, & J. Varacalli, eds., *The Encyclopedia of Catholic Social Thought, Social Science, and Social Policy* (Scarecrow Press, 2007), 388-389.

[32] See Russell Kirk, *The Roots of American Order* (Malibu, Calif.: Pepperdine U. Press, 1974), 61-67.

[33] "Lucius Quinctius Cincinnatus," citing Livy, *Ab Urbe Condita*, iii. 26-29, https://en.wikipedia.org/wiki/Lucius_Quinctius_Cincinnatus; Internet; accessed 25 Dec. 2014.

[34] See, e.g., Christian Wilson, "The American Cincinnatus: The Unique Greatness and Republican Virtue of George Washington," Ashbrook Statesmanship Thesis, http://ashbrook.org/wp-content/uploads/2014/09/Wilson-Printable.pdf; Internet; accessed 25 Dec. 2014.

[35] John Locke, *The Second Treatise of Government* (1690), par. 160.

[36] Edward S. Corwin, *The President: Office and Powers* (N.Y.: New York University Press, 1957), 14, 147-148.

[37] See ibid., 152-154.

[38] Clinton Rossiter, *Constitutional Dictatorship: Crisis Government in the Modern Democracies* (Piscataway, N.J.: Transaction Publishers, 2002 [originally published by Princeton University Press, 1948]).

[39] 570 U.S. ___ (2013).

[40] See Alexander Hamilton, Federalist 78, in Alexander Hamilton, John Jay, & James Madison, *The Federalist* (N.Y.: Random House [Modern Library], n.d.), 504.

[41] *Worcester v. Georgia*, 31 U.S. (6 Pet.) 515 (1832).

[42] See Stephen M. Krason, "Abortion and National Policymaking: Reflections on the Congress Reversing the Rule of *Roe v. Wade* and *Doe v. Bolton*,' in Krason, *The Public Order and the Sacred Order*, 556-557.

[43] Russell Kirk, *The Conservative Constitution* (Washington, D.C.: Regnery Gateway, 1990), 114.

[44] To be sure, the parents in a certain sense got themselves into the unfortunate situation in the first place. They were unwed and the father shook the baby when she was fussy and caused her injuries. He has been sentenced to prison for seven years. The mother, who was not home when he did this, was not criminally culpable but the child was placed in foster care (http://www.wmtw.com/news/father-sentenced-to-prison-in-babyshaking-case/29726726; Internet; accessed 21 Dec. 2014). I wrote about this case and about other recent instances where state governors should have exercised strong executive power—or even used basic gubernatorial prerogatives—against overreaching courts and state prosecutors, but regrettably failed to do so in one of my columns (see: "Governors Who Properly Use or Misuse Executive Power," *Crisismagazine.com*, Oct. 28, 2014).

[45] Joshua Rhett Miller, "Maine Governor Orders State to Back Mom in Legal Battle Over Baby's DNR Order," http://www.foxnews.com/us/2014/09/05/maine-mother-fighting-for-abused-daughter-right-to-live-attorneys-say/; Internet; accessed 26 Dec. 2014; Joe Lawlor, "State High Court Dismisses Trask Infant DNR Case," http://www.centralmaine.com/2014/09/19/state-high-court-dismisses-trask-infant-dnr-case/; Internet; accessed 26 Dec. 2014.

[46] Stoyan Zaimov, "NY Cardinal Dolan on Openly Gay NFL Prospect Michael Sam, 'Good for Him, No Judgment,'" http://www.christianpost.com/news/ny-cardinal-dolan-on-openly-gay-nfl-prospect-michael-sam-good-for-him-no-judgment-115883/; Internet; accessed 26 Dec. 2014; Lisa Bourne, "Cardinal Dolan: Debate on Denying Communion to Pro-Abortion Pols 'In the Past,'" *The Jackson Press* (Sept. 28, 2014), http://thejacksonpress. org/?p=25294; Internet; accessed 26 Dec. 2014.

[47] John-Henry Westen, "Chicago's Archbishop Cupich: Communion for Pro-Abortion Politicians Is a Good Thing," *LifeSite News* (Dec. 1, 2014), https://www.life sitenews.com/news/chicagos-archbishop-cupich-communion-for-pro-abortion-politicians -is-a-good; Internet; accessed 28 Dec. 2014.

[48] Rod Dreher, "J. Bottum Flip-Flops on Gay Marriage," *The American Conservative* (Aug. 23, 2013), http://www.theamericanconservative.com/dreher/j-bottum-flip-flops-on-gay-marriage/comment-page-1/; Internet; accessed 26 Dec. 2014.

[49] Marc Santora, "Gay Groups to March in St. Patrick's Day Parade as Ban Falls," *The New York Times* (Sept. 3, 2014), http://www.nytimes.com/2014/09/04/nyregion/new-york-st-patricks-day-parade-organizers-lift-ban-on-gay-groups.html?_r=0; Internet; accessed 26 Dec. 2014; Mark Pratt, "Gay Vets Can March in Boston St. Patrick's Day Parade" (Dec. 16, 2014), http://abcnews.go.com/US/wireStory/gay-veterans-bostons-st-patricks-day-parade-27 628958; Internet; accessed 26 Dec. 2014.

[50] Robert Royal recently made this point about how some are advising the bishops to focus on evangelization and give up on opposing same-sex "marriage" (Joan Desmond, "The Catholic Church and Same-Sex Marriage: Time for Retreat?" *The National Catholic Register*, Dec. 14, 2014; http://www.ncregister.com/blog/joan-desmond/the-catholic-church-and-same-sex-marriage-time-for-a-truce-or-a-new-strateg; Internet; accessed, 22 Dec. 2014.

[51] "Chicago's Archbishop Cupich Will Not Deny Pro-Choice Politicians Communion, Emphasizes Dialogue," by Carol Kuruvilla, http://www.huffingtonpost.com/2014/12/01/chicago-archbishop-cupich-communion_n_6249544.html; Internet; accessed 22 Dec. 2014.

[52] Paul Hanly Furfey, *The Mystery of Iniquity* (Milwaukee: Bruce, 1944), 37.

[53] Stephen M. Krason, "Are Church Leaders Unwittingly Promoting a Secularist Agenda?" *Crisismagazine .com* (Oct. 1, 2014).

[54] Ibid.

[55] The importance of a well-formed laity taking the initiative on apologetic efforts is underscored by the insufficiency of catechetics in many American dioceses after Vatican Council II (see, e.g.: Austin V. Vaughan, "Assessment of Present Day Catechesis," in *Teaching the Catholic Faith: Central Questions for the '90s*, ed. Eugene V. Clark [N.Y.: 1991]; Kenneth D. Whitehead, "Catechism of the Catholic Church" in *The Encyclopedia of Catholic Social Thought, Social Science, and Social Policy*, 135-137). That the problem persists in some dioceses is seen in comments recently by Raymond L. Cardinal Burke (see: "Cardinal Burke Offers Insights on the Synod on the Family and the New Evangelization" [interview with Don Fier], *The Wanderer* [Jan. 8, 2015], 3A).

[56] See *The Transformation of the American Democratic Republic*, 435-436. Robert Royal points out how in 1976, Henry Kissinger—who was at the very pinnacle of the

U.S. foreign policy establishment at the time—said, "The day of the United States is past and today is the day of the Soviet Union. My job as Secretary of State is to negotiate the most acceptable second-best position available."

[57] I mention in a footnote in *The Transformation of the American Democratic Republic* (499) two small anecdotes that I witnessed as a graduate student in the last decade of the Cold War that indicated this decline of the hold of Communist ideology right in the very epicenter of that worldwide ideology, the Soviet Union. One was when a graduate school colleague mentioned that a Russian exile friend of his—another graduate student, who had been one of the Russian Jewish émigrés from the U.S.S.R. in the 1970s—had talked about the steep decline of Communist ideology in his former country. The other was when the exiled Soviet dissident journalist and poet Aleksandr Ginzburg gave a lecture on campus, at the State University of New York at Buffalo. During the question-and-answer period after the talk, one member of the audience asked Ginzburg how many Communists there were in the Soviet Union. He replied—through an interpreter—that there were none; they were all in places like France and the U.S.

Index

About the Contributors

Allan C. Carlson is President of the Howard Center, Editor of *Family in America*, and International Secretary of the World Congress on Families. A leading scholar on the family, his books have included *Family Questions: Reflections on the American Social Crisis, The American Way: Family and Community in the Shaping of the American Identity,* and *The Swedish Experiment in Family Politics*. He has taught at Hillsdale College and Oriel College, Oxford.

Anthony Esolen is Professor of English at Providence College. He is a frequent contributor to *The Claremont Review of Books, Touchstone,* and *Crisis Magazine*, and also author of *The Politically Incorrect Guide to Western Civilization.*

Anne Hendershott is Professor of Sociology and Director of the Veritas Center for Ethics in Public Life at Franciscan University of Steubenville. Her books have included *The Politics of Deviance*, *The Politics of Abortion*, and *Status Envy: The Politics of Catholic Higher Education.*

James Kalb is a lawyer, independent scholar, frequent contributor to *Crisis Magazine*, and author of *The Tyranny of Liberalism* and *Against Inclusiveness.*

Stephen M. Krason is Professor of Political Science and Legal Studies, Director of the Political Science Program, and Associate Director of the Veritas Center for Ethics in Public Life at Franciscan University of Steubenville. He is also Editor of the Religion and Society Book Series of Franciscan University Press, co-founder and president of the Society of Catholic Social Scientists, and a lawyer. His books have included *The Transformation of the American Democratic Republic* and *The Public Order and the Sacred Order.*

Sheila Liaugminas is an Emmy Award-winning journalist formerly with *Time Magazine*, who has extensive experience in both the secular and Catholic media. She is host of *A Closer Look* on Relevant Radio and author of *Non-Negotiable: Essential Principles of a Just Society and Humane Culture.*

Robert R. Reilly is a former presidential assistant, diplomat, and Director of Voice of America and author of *Making Gay Okay: How Rationalizing Homosexual Behavior Is Changing Everything.*

Lawrence M. Stratton is Director of the Stover Center for Constitutional Studies and Moral Leadership and Assistant Professor of Ethics and Constitutional Law at Waynesburg University. He is also a lawyer, ordained minister in the Presbyterian Church (U.S.A.), and co-author of *The Tyranny of Good Intentions: How Prosecutors and Law Enforcement Are Trampling the Constitution in the Name of Justice*.

Duncan Stroik is a noted architect and Professor of Architecture at the University of Notre Dame. He is also founder of the Institute for Sacred Architecture and founding editor of the *Sacred Architecture Journal*.

Benjamin Wiker is Associate Professor of Political Science and Human Life Studies and senior fellow of the Veritas Center for Ethics in Public Life at Franciscan University of Steubenville. He is the author of numerous books, including *Ten Books that Screwed Up the World* and *Worshipping the State*.